I0220644

Frederic Mayer Bird

Lutheran Hymnology

Frederic Mayer Bird

Lutheran Hymnology

ISBN/EAN: 9783337038700

Printed in Europe, USA, Canada, Australia, Japan

Cover: Foto ©Lupo / pixelio.de

More available books at **www.hansebooks.com**

THE

EVANGELICAL
QUARTERLY REVIEW.

NO. LXI

JANUARY, 1865.

ARTICLE III.

LUTHERAN HYMNOLOGY.

By Rev. FREDERIC M. BIRD, A. M., Philadelphia.

THE present article proposes to deal neither with the abundant treasures of original German hymnology, nor with the narrow field occupied by such sacred verses as individuals of our communion may have written in the English language. The former subject would require a volume, the latter would scarcely admit a paragraph. Our business is with such Hymn Books as the Church, or her members have published "for the use, edification, and comfort" of such of the flock as are American born, or thoroughly anglicized. Of these English hymnals there are, or have been, more than people in general are aware, and of them in succession we shall aim to give accounts as fair and full as they may deserve, or the readers of the *Quarterly* desire.

The City of New York took the lead in this business. Comparing the present with the past, it is not encouraging to know that the Lutheran Church or churches in that city were wealthy, active, and liberal enough to publish for themselves successively, between the years 1795 and 1806, *three* English hymn books. Of these volumes, which are all interesting and important to the lover of our Church literature and history, the two earlier are very scarce, and the last by no means common. Dr. Reynolds, writing on this subject in the Review for October, 1859, devoted three pages

to the first of these compilations, but was unacquainted with
its successors. The present writer has them all bodily before
him, and aims to set their spirit, at least, before his readers.

Dr. Kunze's Hymn Book. 1795. 240 *Hymns.*

The title page reads: "A Hymn and Prayer Book : For
the Use of such Lutheran Churches, as use the English Language. Collected by John C. Kunze, D. D., Senior of the
Lutheran Clergy in the State of New York. Coll. 3 : 16,
Teaching and admonishing one another in Psalms. New
York : Printed and sold by Hurtin & Commardinger, No.
450. Pearl Street, [with privilege of copy-right,] 1795."

The book, (also its two successors,) is a very little larger
than the common edition of the well-known collection of the
New York Synod, (of which we shall speak hereafter,) and
is printed with about the same sized type. The Preface covers three pages, and contains some interesting historical matter. 300 pages are occupied with the hymns, and 163 by
the Liturgical and other prose matter, containing the Liturgy, the Epistles and Gospels for the year, Luther's Shorter
Catechism, "Fundamental Questions," "The Order of Salvation," "The Christian Duties," (these three cover 13 pages.)
A short account of the Christian Religion ; a short account
of the Lutheran Church; the seven Penitential Psalms, and
some forms of Prayer. Much of this matter merits description, if only for its antiquity and curiousness ; but this is not
the place to present it. We return to our hymns, which are
arranged as follows : (I copy from the table of contents.)

1. On Advent and Christmas, hymn 1 ; 2. New Year, 16 ;
3. Lent, 22 ; 4. Easter, 46 ; 5. Ascension, 51 ; 6. Whit
Sunday, 54 ; 7. Trinity, 59 ; 8. Creation and Providence, 63 ;
9. Redemption, 72 ; 10. Justifying Faith, 88 ; 11. Word of
God, 121 ; 12. Catechisation, 123 ; 13. Baptism, 126 ; 14.
Lord's Supper, 128 ; 15. Sanctification, 141 ; 16. Praise of
God, 172 ; 17. Morning, 190 ; 18. Evening, 193 ; 19. Com-
plaints and Consolation, 201 ; 20. Prayer and Intercession,
207 ; 21. Funeral Occasions, 210 ; 22. Different Matter in
an Appendix, 221.

Next, for the origin of these hymns. The Preface says :
"Most all of the hymns are translations from the German,
and were used before in their churches. All except those
in the appendix are taken from printed books, particularly
the German Psalmody, printed in London and re-printed in
New York, by H. Gaine, 1756, with which many serious

English persons have been greatly delighted; and from an excellent collection of the Moravian Brethren, printed in London, 1789. In the appendix only 1 have taken the liberty to add a few of my own, and of the Rev. Messrs. Ernst's and Strebeck's, both translations and original compositions." Of the twenty separate productions in this "Appendix," six have the initial of Dr. Kunze, five, of his assistant Strebeck, and four, of Ernst: No. 238 is the "Litteny," in prose; 240 is "Watts' Cradle Hymn; 239 "The Golden Alphabet;" happily anonymous, while two metrical mongrels which may be called by courtesy hymns bear no initial, but exhibit the same peculiar style of grammar and rhetoric by which this Teutonic trio distinguished themselves in the neighboring pieces. Of the literary character of these compositions we shall speak below.

Of the 220 hymns in the body of the book, 70 appear to be of English origin. Watts supplies 13, Charles Wesley 7, Newton 4, Hart 3, Cowper 2. Kerr 2, Hammond 2, Doddridge, Steele, Toplady, Mason, Wesley, Sr., Erskine, Mrs. Palmer, and Langford, each one, and 11 are anonymous. (This is our own computation; author's names are nowhere indicated, except in the appendix with the few hymns marked K. S., and E.) And 13 more, which are found in the Moravian Collection of 1789, appear to be of English Moravian origin.

The remaining 150 hymns are translated from the German: three of them by John Wesley, the rest by anonymous Moravian writers. 75 are taken from the aforementioned book of 1789: the rest are doubtless all from the Psalmodia Germanica, published in 1756 and earlier. Of that curious and important work the present writer, unfortunately neither possesses nor has seen a copy: he is thus unable to verify the origin of nearly one-third of Dr. Kunze's hymns. But it seems probable that Dr. Kunze neither owned, nor used to any extent, any other English hymnals than the two mentioned; for most of the purely English hymns, Watts', Wesley's, and the rest, are found in the Moravian book of 1789. We are safe, therefore, in fathering the seventy-odd hymns, not otherwise accounted for, upon the Psalmodia Germanica, of which J. C. Jacobi was the chief translator.

The Psalmodia Germanica is supposed by Dr. Reynolds to have been a Lutheran rather than a Moravian work. In that case the translations in Dr. Kunze's book are derived in

equal parts from Lutheran and Moravian sources. But very
many of the English Moravian renderings are made from
Lutheran sources, especially Gerhardt; so that (what has
occured in no subsequent English hymnal,) *more than half
the contents are of Lutheran origin.*

The literary merit of these contents, of course, varies
greatly. Some few verses are excellent, more are respectable, most are indifferent and negative, while several are better adapted to kindle mirth than devotion. The original
English hymns, for the most part, are neither the best, nor the
worst of their kind. Of the translated lyrics, perhaps half
are in the irregular German metres, not easily singable out
of their native tongue : the rest are L. M., C. M., and
other familiar measures. The opening verses of the volume,
and many afterwards, go smoothly enough to have been acceptable, 70 years ago :

Now the Saviour comes indeed,   To the wonder of mankind,
Of the virgin mother's seed,   By the Lord himself designed.

Not a few of the hymns flow with a strong, if rough, cur-
rent, and begin with most vigorous and startling bursts of
sense and sound, thus No. 54 :

"Retake thy own possesion, Thou glorious guest of hearts !"

Hymn 128 :

"Trim thy lamp, O soul betrothed !"

Hymn 142 :

Storms and winds may blow and batter Deem these trials no great matter,
   Nay life's vessel overwhelm :   For our Saviour guides the helm."

Hymn 98 :

How bright appears the morning star,
With grace and truth beyond com- The royal root of Jesse !"
   pare,

Several of our noblest and most famous German hymns
are rendered with some appreciation and force ; though we
can do better by them now. Here is the first verse from :

"Ein' feste Burg :"

"God is our refuge in distress,   Th' infernal enemy,
Our strong defence and armor,   Look ! how enraged is he !
He's present, when we're comfortless, He now exerts his force
In storms He is our harbor :   To stop the gospel-course ;
                                    Who can withstand this tyrant ?"

And from the not less glorious:

"Befiehl du deine Wege:"

"Commit thy ways and goings,
And all that grieves thy soul,
To Him whose wisest doings,
Rule all without control.

He makes the times and seasons,
Revolve from year to year,
And knows ways, means, and seasons,
When help shall best appear."

And from that unequalled Passion-hymn:

"O Haupt, voll Blut und Wunden:"

"O Head so full of bruises,
So full of pain and scorn,
Midst other sore abuses,
Mocked with a crown of thorn!
          *   *   *   *   *
O what a consolation
Doth in my heart take place.

When I thy toil and passion,
Can in some measure trace!
     *   *   *   *   *
Ah, then, though I be dying,
Midst sickness, grief and pain,
I shall, on thee relying,
Eternal life obtain."

One or two of these translations of particular hymns have never yet been surpassed, and are almost, or quite worthy to be used at this day. Witness this from Angelus:

"Liebe die du mich zum Bilde:"

"Lord thine image Thou hast lent me,
In thy never-fading love:
I was fall'n: but Thou hast sent me

Full redemption from above.
Sacred Love, I long to be
Thine to all eternity."

And the following, of Zinzendorf:

"Welcome among thy flock of grace
With joyful acclamation;
Thou whom our Shepherd we confess,
Come, feed thy congregation.

Who owns the doctrine of thy cross
To be her sole foundation.
Accept from every one of us
The deepest adoration."

And from a judgment-hymn by Ringwalt, the last verse:

"Es ist gewisslich eine Zeit:"

"O Jesu, shorten thy delay,
And hasten thy salvation.
That we may see that glorious day
Produce a new creation.

O come, O Lord, our Judge and King!
Come, change our mournful notes,
to sing
Thy praise forever. Amen."

This is one side of the shield: there are enough examples of the other. Thus hymn 71:

"Why should I continue grieving? *Ha'n't* I still Christ my hill," etc.

Likewise hymn 68:

"Jehovah, thy wise government,
And its administration,

Is found to be most excellent,
On due consideration."

But the most remarkable models of English metrical composition which the book affords, are the originals in the Appendix. Dr. Reynolds, in his article five years ago, gave three of these, and the printer succeeded in making them worse than they are in the volume. One sample will suffice now. The following stupendous production stands No. 222, is headed "A Church Hymn," and tailed "K." It runs through 12 verses:

4. "We called thy bride drawn to thy sight
   King, by thy ointment's savor,
   Lay at thy feet, and pray, to meet
   A glimpse of kindly favor.

7. Lord it is gain here to remain,
   These pews yield milk and honey
   Brooks for the hart, nests for the bird,
   Rocks for the frightened coney.

9. I shut my ears to worldly cares
   And to the roaring lion,

And at heaven's gate anticipate
   The rest of holy Zion.

11. Thy sceptre's top if touched, will stop
   The torrent of wild notions,
   And hearts of stone will melt and own
   The fruit of joined devotions.

12. We mingle here with tears our cheer,
   Yet candidates of glory,
   Unmixt will be our psalmody
   In realms not transitory..'

Whoever will studiously examine the above, will eventually discover, that it is not such nonsense as it seems, and that there is even some poetry in it. But the light of the ideas (which are not bad) is certainly hid under a bushel of bad English.

A few remarks on the general character of Dr. Kunze's volume will finish this the most difficult section of our subject. The book, as might be expected from the above statement of the sources whence its contents are drawn, bears not a little resemblance to the Moravian hymnals. Those curious collections, from first to last, have the same character and tone: and it is an open question whether the present manual of the United Brethren is an improvement on their immense and famous tome of 1745. It has commonly been the fate of our English hymnbooks in this country to be rather something else than Lutheran. Just as the New York collection was supposed to be a cross between high Arianism, and a mild loose form of cosmopolite old-style orthodoxy, and as the various editions of the General Synod have presented an agreeable mixture, in varying proportions, of Methodism and New School Presbyterianism, relieved by a gentle tincture of our own faith, so it was the luck of Dr. Kunze's product to come into the world with an evident Moravian flavor. The metres, the grammar, the style, the tone of thought and feeling, all have a smack of *Unitas Fratrum.* The visible and tangible blood of Christ does not flow through the book so palpably, as in those from which it is compiled, but there is more of it on the surface than we usually find in non-Moravian volumes. "Besprinkle with thy blood my heart :" "O tell me often of each wound :" "The enjoyment of Christ's flesh and blood :" lines like these are frequent. Yet to the manner and extent of this, exception can be taken on the score of taste only, not of doctrine. The more serious extravagances of the Moravians are pruned away ; the carnalizing of sacred things, so frequent among them, is carefully avoided ; and the matter and spirit of the book are Lutheran. The arrangement is, in the main, good. The Church itself is not brought forward as it should be, but the great Festivals are worthily emphasized, and Baptism and Catechisation (which together may include the head of Confirmation), with the Lord's Supper, are made prominent. "Justifying Faith" is the nearest approach which has yet been made, so far as we know, in any English Hymn Book, to the ideal title, "Faith and Justification :" and this and "Sanctification" between them, give a much more scriptural, churchly, and convenient order than the awkward lumbering length. to which our modern books are so much attached, of promiscuous "Christian Experience." Taken all in all, Dr. Kunze's work is not the least creditable which the Lutheran Church in America has brought forth. The Tennessee and Ohio books may be more positively churchly, (for its prevailing tone is subjective and mildly pietistic,) but we doubt if they are much better, in general. And if we allow for the remote time and the peculiar circumstances, remembering that the book was gotten up by one or two isolated German clergymen just beginning to use English, and necessarily unacquainted, to any considerable extent, either with the language or its hymnology, we shall see that good Dr. Kunze did his work better, in proportion to his abilities and oportunities, than most who have followed him. His book may be faulty, but the authors of none of the English Lutheran hymnbooks now in use, have a right to be complacent over its defects. When we shall have a Hymnal, at once, as sound in doctrine and spirit as this, which at the same time corresponds to, and bears evidence of, the immense advances that have been, or

might have been made, in taste and knowlenge, since 1795,
we shall then be justified in criticising the first English Lutheran Hymn Book. Meantime we may remember, that all
things have small beginnings : and that the venerated man,
who laid this corner-stone of an edifice, destined to be long
in the building, straggling in its shape, and vastly various in
the fitness, use, and beauty of its numerous chambers, did it
in love and loyalty, though somewhat in the dark.

Strebeck's Collection, 1797. 299 *Hymns.*

Size and appearance similar to the last : it is labelled on
the back, "Hymns and Liturgy." Title : "A collection of
Evangelical Hymns, made from different authors and collections, for the English Lutheran Church, in New York : By
George Strebeck : and when they had sung an hymn, they
went out into the Mount of Olives, Mat. 26 : 30. New York :
Printed by John Tiebout, (Horner's Head). No. 358, Pearl
street, 1797." The preface, or advertisement, covers a
page and a quarter, and is signed September, 1797. It
says, "As this small collection of hymns is published for the
use of my own congregation, and by its particular request,
it needs no apology. The unsuitableness of the metres of our
English Lutheran Hymn Book, published in 1795, * * * *
made it peculiarly necessary to provide another collection for
the use of the English Lutheran Church. In the present
collection, I have endeavored to retain as many of the hymns,
published in the former, as could well be done. All those
have this mark * prefixed to them ; for the rest I am indebt-
ed to various authors, and collections of reputation. I hope
none will be so bigoted to *mere name* as to censure us for
making selections from authors who are not of our own pro-
fession in religion ; and who, perhaps, on some points differ
from us in sentiment," etc. The hymns and index cover
263 pages ; with them are bound up "The Liturgy, Gospels,
and Epistles, of the English Lutheran Church of New York ;
to which is added, the Augustan Confession of Faith. New
York (as before), 1797." This covers 130 pages.

Here is "A table of contents. I. The Nativity of Christ,
from page 1–20. II. New Year, 21–22. III. Christ's
sufferings and death, 29–51. IV. Easter ; or the resurrection, 51–60. V. Ascension, 60–64. VI. Whitsunday, or
the Holy Spirit. (I keep the book's lettering as to capitals
or not, 65–74. VII. Trinity Sunday. 74–80. VIII. Crea-

tion, 81–89. IX. Divine Providence, 90–100. X. Redemption, 100–110. XI. Repentance, 110–126. XII. Faith, 126–137. XIII. Sanctification, 137–146. XIV. Means of Grace; 1 The Scriptures, 146–162 : 2 Baptism, 162–165 : 3 The Lord's Supper, 165–179 : 4 Prayer, 179–199. XV. Praise, 200–207. XVI. Death, 207–220. XVII. Judgment, 221–229. XVIII. 1 Heaven, 230–234 : 2 Hell, 235–236. XIX. 1 Morning, 236–239 : 2 Evening, 239–241. XX. Miscellaneous subjects, 241–254.

Here is a falling off in doctrine and churchliness at the very start. The precious season of *Advent* is passed by, our preparation for Christ is neglected, and his coming taken as a matter of course, in the simple acknowledgment of his *nativity*. And presently appears the common and pernicious error of confounding the full and proper Means *of* Grace with such things as are, or may be means *to* grace. The Word and Sacraments, which are God's means toward men, are put on the same footing with Prayer, which is our means towards him. Of course this mixture and leveling of causes with ,results, of divine with human, though popular enough even in the Church, is totally inconsistent with the Lutheran doctrine. Mr. Strebeck had been one of Dr. Kunze's assistants, had some hand, it will be remembered, in making the hymnbook which his own in part supplanted. But he seems, in these two years intervening, to have taken (doubtless unconsciously) several steps towards what then happily had not yet a local habitation and a name—American Lutheranism. He afterwards, with his congregation and church property, went over to the Episcopalians.

Of the hymns, 299 in number, 48 only are taken from Dr. Kunze's book ; and of these but ten, with three others by John Wesley, are translated from the German. This is a great and sudden change ; but it is in human nature to pass violently from one extreme to another. The contents of the first book were two-thirds of German origin : in the second, published but two years later, Fatherland was allowed to publish but one-twenty-third. Of the English hymns, Watts has supplied 82 ; Charles Wesley 45 ; Newton 18 ; Doddridge 17 ; Cowper 11 ; Steele 11 ; the Stennets 8 ; Beddome 7 ; Hart 5 ; Fawcet, Medley, Davies, and Burnhaw 3 each ; Addison, Mason, Toplady, Gibbons, Stocker, Swain, Turner, 2 each ; and authors various and anonymous the remainder.

The book, thus constituted, has no special character of its

own. and presents no further claims on our attention ; unless
in introducing four doxologies, where Dr. Kunze had none,
in affixing the authors names to nearly half the hymns. and
in containing, entire and unaltered, John Wesley's noble
translation of "*Befiehl du deine Wege.*" Its literary merit
is passable. for that day. even good. Some 80 of the hymns
are such as a severe, and as many more such as an ordinary, taste would retain. As far as it goes. it is for its date a
respectable production ; and we know a number of standard
collections in use now, that are not much better.

Williston's Collection. 1806. 437 *Hymns.*

It is now our pleasant duty to describe a book of decided
character and considerable merit. Its page is a thought larger than the last, and better printed, the label on the back is
the same, "Hymns and Liturgy." Title : "A Choice Selection of Evangelical Hymns, from various Authors ; for the
use of the English Evangelical Lutheran Church in New
York. By Ralph Williston. I will sing with the Spirit,
and I will sing with the understanding also 1 Cor. 14 : 15.
New York : Printed and sold by J. C. Totten, No. 155
Chatham Street, 1806." The book is copy-righted ; this occupies the page succeeding the Title. The next is filled by
an official statement signed "John C. Kunze. Senior of the
Lutheran Clergy in the State of New York, N. Y., Feb. 20,
1806," beginning : "The Evangelical Lutheran Ministry of
this State having entered a resolution some years ago, *That
a new edition of the English Lutheran Hymn-Book should
be procured,* and having left the selection of the Hymns to
the members of their body residing in the city of New York,
this collection is now offered," etc., and ending : "I have examined and read every one of the Hymns now offered, before
their being struck off, and can assure my fellow-worshippers,
that none is found among them dissonant to our doctrine, or
incompatible with the spirit of genuine godliness." From
this it appears that the book before us is a properly authorized Church collection, whereas Strebeck's was a private affair, for the use merely of his own congregation. On the
third page from the Title appears the compiler's "advertisement." It is not pretended, that a Hymn will be found here
adapted to every religious subject, yet it is hoped there will
be no important deficiency. No doctrine, it is believed, will
be found in this selection, which is not accordant with the
doctrines taught in our Church. A new edition. or a new

compilation, became indispensably necessary, there not being a single copy to be had of the former collection ; and the obvious deficiency of the former collection determined us to make a new compilation." The hymns and index occupy 319 pages, to which are in some copies added, as in Strebeck, in 100 pages more, "The Liturgy, Gospels and Epistles of the English Evangelical Lutheran Church in New York."

The arrangement is more minute and somewhat more logical than Strebeck's, but not more Churchly. Contents : I. The Being and Perfections of God, page 1 ; II. The Character, Actions, Sufferings and Glory of Christ: 1 Nativity, p. 13 ; 2, Officers, 26 ; 3 Passion, 36 ; 4 Resurrection, 61 ; 5 Ascension, 67 ; 6 Glory, 71 ; 7 Advocacy, 76. III. Influences of the Spirit of God : 1 Whitsunday, 81 ; 2 Trinity, 95, (this is a curious coupling.) IV. 1 Creation, 102 ; 2 Providence, 108. V. The Fall and Temptation of Man, 122. VI. The Scriptures, Doctrines and Imitations of the Scriptures : 1 The Scriptures, 126 ; 2 Doctrinal, 133 ; 3 Inviting, 145. VII. The Christian's Character and Graces : 1 Awakening, 152 ; 2 Penitential, 158 ; 3 Supplication and Prayer, 173 ; 4 Faith, 196 ; 5 Hope, 203 ; 6 Love, 207 ; 7 Sanctification, 217 ; 8 Joy and Praise, 224. VIII. The Christian's Blessings, Sufferings, Danger and Safety, 233. IX. Christian Worship : 1 Private, 245 ; 2 Public, 247. X. Pastoral, 260. XI. Ordinances : 1 Baptism, 267 ; 2 Eucharistic, 269. XII. Times, Seasons and Places : 1 Morning, 273 : 2 Evening, 275 ; 3 Birthday, 278 ; 4 Youth, 280 ; 5 New Year. 280 ; 6 Seasons, 286 ; 7 Particular Providences, 290 ; 8 Death, 293 ; 9 Resurrection, 299 ; 10 Judgment, 301 ; 11 Heaven, 304.

This arrangement, it will be seen at once, though in no respect positively offensive, is, like its predecessors, and increasingly so, deficient, weak, negative where it should be positive. The whole plan and temper of the work, indeed, are Presbyterian, Methodist, cosmopolite English, Broad Church, anything else, as much as Lutheran. The authorship of the hymns shows this. The German matter, so largely used by Dr. Kunze, is almost entirely thrown aside. There are eight translations by John Wesley, with the origin of four of which Williston was doubtless unacquainted, and which, we need hardly say, are all vigorous and graceful English poems : and at the end of the Passion hymns are put seven, transferred from Kunze's volume. These last are remarkable for force and feeling, but in rough and unsingable measures : "O head so full of bruises," being the only one of them which an ordinary English congregation could sing now. Of these fifteen hymns, the origin of four only, and they from John Wesley, is indicated, while over two original compositions of Charles Wesley, the same title "[From the German.]" is placed. For the rest, Watts gives 188 hymns, Charles Wesley 112, Steele 17, Doddridge 14, the Stennetts 8, Cowper 7, Newton 5, Addison 4, Hart 4. Beddome 4, Fawcett 3, Browne 3, Davies 3, Tate, Mason, Dwight, Gibbons, Needham, and S. Wesley, Jr., each 2, and the rest a.e various or anonymous. The compiler made no attempt to give the authors' names.

Mr. Williston was a man of fine taste ; and his book possessed, for that day, very unusual literary merit. There is nothing childish, vulgar, or absurd in it, as is so frequently the case with books so old : a modern style and feeling are evident. Almost all its contents are still found in the standard hymnals of respectable religious bodies. A few of them, chiefly from Watts, may be regarded as not quite fitting with the idea and objects of a hymn for public worship, nor likely to result in edification ; but these most objectionable parts of the collection still have place in many modern manuals. Taken in all, Williston's book will endure comparison, so far as it goes, with almost any of those now used ; which, to be sure, is no great praise,. At the time, it was doubtless superior to anything else printed in America, and was perhaps hardly surpassed in England, except by that wonderful production, John Wesley's great Hymn Book "for the use of the people called Methodists." From that liberal source Williston drew largely ; and he must also have possessed one or more of the comparatively rare original volumes from which that was compiled : for his book contains several Wesleyan hymns which were then, as now, out of print generally and forgotten. Wherever Charles Wesley's lyrics are, there will be as much vigor and grace as has yet been put into Christian poetry. His brother's verses, comparatively few in number, are nearly equal to Charles' best : and 120 Wesleyan hymns, in a volume containing but 437, necessarily give it tone, force, and vitality. We do not sanction the *doctrine* of the book by saying that its poetic and devotional character is high ; and 120 Wesleyan hymns, as loosely chosen as was to be expected at that day and from Mr. Williston's position, necessarily infuse more or less of a spirit which is anything but Lutheran. (When non-Methodists, since that time, have taken from the Wesleyan poetry to an extent at all proportionate to its merits, their selections have not commonly been much more careful or appropriate.) But Williston's Hymn Book is the most praiseworthy, in literary and poetic merit, which has yet been issued by the Lutheran Church, and it is deeply to be lamented, that in the labors of his successors, his own were so almost utterly disregarded.

It seems to have been the fashion, among these early hymnals, for each compiler to ignore, as near as might be, what had been done before him. If the getters-up of the official New York collection had been content to build on the basis of Williston, keeping what was good in him, rejecting what was objectionable, and adding what appeared desirable, a volume might have been produced which would have met the wants of the great bulk of English Lutheran churches for many years, and been vastly superior to anything which we have now. For Williston had unconsciously hit upon the first requisite of a good English hymn book ; the presence of Watts and Wesley in nearly equal proportions. This is a secret which was partially understood sixty years ago, but has been unhappily forgotten since. The collections that appeared through the closing years of the last century and at the beginning of this, have generally a much larger infusion of Wesley than happens in later days, and the consequence is a spice, and a definiteness, *vim* and life, that are unknown to our languid and rambling piles of verse. Wesley and Watts are, and will doubtless always remain, *par excellence* the hymnists of the English tongue. Their provinces are different, and they seldom cover the same ground ; never with the same material or in the same manner. As *poets* there is no comparison between them, as purveyors to the wants of public worship they are nearly equal. Watts is the more practical and popular, Wesley the more cultivated, graceful, and profound, also the more fiery, inspired and inspiring. They are needed to complete each other ; two sides of the shield, old and new school ; and truth and value in each. The Presbyterian gives the hymns of praise and worship, of outward duty and service, the objective side of Christianity ; the Methodist deals with repentance, faith, consecration, and inward sanctity ; the whole range of hidden life and experience, more or less personal and subjective. Can we dispense with, or undervalue either ? Each of these two gifted and holy men has done his work better than any other ; can we, in

justice to them and to ourselves, throw either in the shade ?
Moreover, it is commonly forgotten that Charles Wesley,
with all his Methodism, was a strenuous and zealous churchman ; his views of the Church, the Sacraments, the Festivals, were nearer ours than those of any other English hymnist of eminence ; and his verses, more or less often, express
these views worthily and nobly.   All the Calvinistic hymn
books in this country have Watts in enormous bulk, and
shave down Wesley to shameful littleness.   Our own compilations all in the same way, though not quite to the same extent.   Williston's was the solitary and noble exception ; that
discerning man established a precedent, which the Church, to
her own infinite loss, has lacked the knowledge, or wit, or
grace, to keep and follow.   When a hymn book that shall
worthily represent both our Lutheran truth and the riches of
English hymology shall appear, it will be much nearer in this
respect to Williston's than to any other of the many compilations which, for want of better, the Lutheran Church in
America has used, and is using.

The New York Synod's Hymn Book. 1814. 520 *hymns.*

But Williston's successors did not see matters in this light.
Six years after his book was published, the New York Synod
had a local habitation and a name, and the tide of Rationalism
had swept into it with considerable power.   Our business here
is not to be philosophical, pathetic, censorious, or apologetic
about the facts, but simply to state them ; "only this and
nothing more."   If anybody is hurt, it is not our fault : we
did not make the facts, and we are not responsible for them.
If we, Lutheran clergymen of the present day, had lived at
that time and under those influences, probably we should
have been as the fathers in New York were, or possibly we
might not.   But this is neither here nor there.   So it was,
and the chronicler, who in his straight course comes against
the facts, has nothing to do but state them dispassionately in
their various bearings and results, so far as these concern his
work and his end.   We may suppose that the representative
men of that day, who made the New York Hymn Book, without being specially tied down to Lutheran doctrine, or remarkably attached to Lutheran forms, or profoundly impreg-
nated with Lutheran spirit, had a sort of instinctive and in-
herited attachment to the Lutheran Church as such ; and
that they were equally displeased with Mr. Williston's evangelical creed and temper, and with his apostasy (as they may

have considered it) to the Church of Christ under another name. At any rate, they practically ignored him and his book; and refer to him and his predecessors only in one slight and sweeping clause of their Preface. "This (the compilation of an English Hymn Book) has indeed already been attempted by several individuals. But as the selections, published by them, evidently admit of great improvement, another was ordered to be prepared by a Committee appointed for that purpose by the Lutheran Synod of the State of New York, convened at Rhinebeck in September, A. D., 1812." This Preface is signed by Dr. Quitman, President, and Dr. Wackerhagen, Secretary, of the Synod: it is not stated who composed the Committee, and as the Minutes of Synod were not printed, prior to 1820, it is now difficult, if not impossible, to ascertain who were the compilers of the book. It has been generally understood that Dr. Mayer "was to a very great extent, if not altogether its author; and the fact of his being the only English scholar belonging to the Synod at that time, is a strong corroboration." So writes Dr. Pohlman, now and, for many years, President of the New York Synod. We are inclined to think, however, that Dr. Quitman, who was the intellectual giant of that time and region, whose influence over New York Lutheranism during the first quarter of this century was commanding, exercised more or less modifying and expurgating power, either during the compilation, or before it went to press. Dr. Quitman's humanitarianism is commonly supposed to have been stronger than Dr. Mayer is ever likely to have been fiavored with, even in his earliest days.

Be this as it may, the book is before us. As every Lutheran minister, who knows or cares anything about our hymnology, is likely to possess and be familiar with this collection, the minute description which we gave of its rare and generally unknown predecessors would be needless here. We have therefore only to state the main facts about the book, and enter into such criticism of it as may seem desirable.

But two varieties in form were ever published: the 18 mo. printed in New York and Philadelphia, from 1814 to the present day, and commonly used: and the 24 mo. put forth in Germantown, by M. Billmeyer. This edition was extensively circulated at first, but went out of print many years ago. The paging in the two is different: the large style having 350 pages of Hymns and 15 of Index, with 153 of Liturgy and Prayers: and the small one 293, 13 and 116 respectively. The collection speedily came into general use among the English churches, of Pennsylvania, as well as New York, and kept its hold for many years. With the Supplement (to be described hereafter,) it is still used in Albany, New York city, Easton, Reading, in half a dozen country churches in New York and New Jersey, and perhaps in a few more in Pennsylvania.

It is the common luck of things and people to be either under-rated or over-praised: the New York Collection has doubtless met both fates. Hymn Books, like human beings, are apt to be at once good and evil ; and this production had great merits and great faults. Let us begin with the bright side.

Its *arrangement* is most lucid and admirable. A clear, strong, sound head presided over this part, as can readily be seen. The subjects follow and flow into each other, in an order, logical and natural; with nothing but the general Table, it is far easier to find what one wants here, than in the General Synod's book, with its extensive and minute Index of special subjects added. First come, as by right they must, Praise and Thanksgiving ; then the Divine Nature, Works and Providence : then the Church Year in part, indicated nearly as in Williston, by Christ's Mission and Nativity, Office and Mediation, Example, Sufferings and Death, Resurrection and Glory. Then the great omission of the preceding books is remedied by "The Kingdom and Church of Christ." Then comes that left-handed expression of the Pentecostal season, as in Williston, "The Influence of God's Holy Spirit." Trinity, of course, is omitted. Then the Scriptures. Then Prayer, acknowledgement of sin, repentance and conversion. Then the privileges, attributes, and fruits of the new life. Here Christian *Experience* is thrown into the background, and the Christian *Character and Life* brought prominently forward. Part of this would be very right ; but they carried it too far. "Duties of Piety, Personal Duties, Social Duties," are dwelt upon perhaps too much, and the inevitable human heart, in its various stages of discipline under divine grace, acknowledged too little. The General Synod runs wildly to the other extreme, ignoring duty, minutely emphasing all the emotional conditions, methodistically deifying Experience, and seeming scarcely to believe in Life and Character. *In media veritas.* Whoever would pilot the Church to the haven of a true and right Hymnology, must steer between Scylla and Charybdis.

Then the book finishes up with Public Worship, the Sacraments, Particular Occasions, the Troubles of Life, and Last Things.

The only faults of this arrangement are those indicated, and that "Faith" is most loosely and incorrectly represented. Here as in all other books, Lutheran and other, with scarcely an exception, (though not so grossly here, as in many,) the saving, justifying act of belief is confounded with the general Trust to be exercised through life; and that which ought to occupy several exterior subdivisions of the volume is crowded into one small chapter. By remedying these defects, arranging the Order of Salvation and the Christian Life according to Lutheran doctrine and spirit, and making the Church-Year stand out more clearly and positively, the arrangement would become nearly perfect; and the future Hymnals of the Church, if they are to be worthy the name, must build after the general structure of the New York collection.

Another point of great importance in a Hymn Book is its adaptedness to the needs and uses of public worship. In this respect the New York book, as far it goes and within its limits, is good. It is the last, if not the only English Lutheran collection which does all it undertook to do, and is all it aimed to be. What its compilers thought fit that it should contain, is here contained; what they believed in expressing, is here expressed. There is a definiteness, a clearness about it; the book is of its kind a success. It may be faulty and deficient in our eyes or mind, but it suited the wants of that day. What its authors had considered right and aimed at, it became or accomplished: and they and those who thought with them had cause to be contented. Thus there is a certain fitness to practical uses in the book. It doubtless entirely satisfied the ministers and people of those early days, and those who come to use it now, generally form, in course of time, a higher regard for it than they had at first. It is, always within its scope, an admirable book to fit one's services and sermons from: there is a minuteness and preciseness about it, which helps one wonderfully to find what one wants. Of Passion and Atonement hymns there is a lack indeed: you are kept within a certain range: but within that you are amply provided. In the General Synod's book all is loose, and generalizing; if you want a hymn which illustrates a special phase of Trust, Love, Consecration, Sanctification, or one on such an obscure subject as Humility

or Benevolence, you have to plod through nearly the whole
thousand, and then the chances are, three to one, that you
will not find it; but in the New York, if what you want
comes within the scope and plan of the book—you turn to
the place, look over a dozen or two hymns perhaps, and there
it is.   For the sober worship of God's house on the Lord's
day, this production, with all its deficiencies—and we have
no disposition to deny these—is perhaps the best we have.

As to distinctive literary merit, it has been generally allowed much praise.   For that day—a full half century ago—
it deserves much : though its excellencies here are largely
negative.   Like Williston's, it contains little or nothing that
is contemptible ; almost all its contents are decorous, proper,
orderly.   But after Williston's, we sadly miss the force and
fire, the brilliant grace, the life and earnestness, of the large
Wesleyan component.   The book before us is entirely old
school, its authors could not tolerate Methodism, they did
not believe in emotion and enthusiasm to any considerable
extent, religion must be quiet, well-behaved, gentle, dignified
and solemn, and their hymns must be toned down to that
standard.   Now the finest hymns in the language happen to
be of just that sort which they did not care about, or did not
approve of, and when a Collection, on any score of principle, taste or feeling, throws out such material as "Rock of
Ages," "Jesus, Lover of my soul," and "There is a fountain," it deprives itself of the most elegant and forcible sacred poems which have been written.   The heart of the
Church has taken hold of just these subjects : the positive
Divinity of Jesus ; the unqualified Atonement of his blood ;
the possible union, consequent hereupon, between man and
God ; and the ideal duties and privileges of the new life.
The best sacred poetry, whether it be objective or subjective,
dealing either with the outward facts, or the inward experience, of religion, is necessarily ardent, intense, often pas-
sionate, sometimes rapturous.   The authors of the New
York collection did not believe in this kind, and that belief
or unbelief inevitably prevented their book from possessing
the highest literary, as the highest devotional, excellence.
Yet within the limits which their principles prescribed, they
did their work remarkably well.   Of its kind, the book is as
good as could well be put together at that day; far better,
in its scope, than most that have a larger scope.   The sacred
muse does not grovel here, as we are so often pained to see
her do in more modern manuals; she may not reach the

same heights of inspiration with the more distinctively evangelical sisters, but she does not s nk to the degraded depths
in which they sometimes repose ; she may prune Dr. Watts
of a noble verse like

"Was it for crimes that I had done, He groaned upon the tree ?"

and forbid him on her premises to

"Survey the wondrous cross,   On which the Prince of Glory died ;"

but neither does she allow him to meditate

"My heart how dreadful hard it is ! Heavy and cold within my breast,
How heavy here it lies !   Just like a rock of ice."

The book belongs entirely to the old school of hymnology
and of piety. Watts gives it the best part of two hundred
hymns ; Doddridge, some seventy or eighty ; Anne Steele
near fifty ; the Stennets, Gibbons, Needham, Browne, Thomas Scott, Beddome, and writers of that sort are extensively
represented ; while Charles Wesley is reduced to a beggarly
compliment ; and his few followers gain scanty and suspicious
admission. Yet there are one or two happy exceptions ; in
several of John Wesley's German hymns, whose exquisite
and noble beauty forced for them a passage. Besides "Give
to the winds thy fears," which, being about Providence merely, might come in easily enough, we find three verses of a
very sweet, decidedly inward and somewhat pietistic production of Terstugen, "Thou hidden love of God ;" five of that
noble hymn of uncertain origin, "O Thou to whose all-search-
ing sight ;" and four of Rothe's sublime song, "Now I have
found the ground wherein." The General Synod's book,
which seems to have been principled against printing anything from the German in a form fit to sing, of course omit-
ed these. It is not the most creditable among the minor
features of that compilation, that having this magnificent
version to its hand, it substituted the spiritless imitation of
Dr. Mills.

Though we have endeavored to be systematic, and to reserve
the *doctrine* of the book to a place by itself, it has inevitably been touched upon, in the above remarks. Dr. Reynolds' criticisms on this subject, in the Review for October,
1859, are tolerably correct. He says, in substance, (page
190) that the essential doctrines of orthodox Christianity do
find expression here, and that the New York collection contains hymns and verses which are inconsistent with Arianism,

Socinianism, or any other heresy. Had this never been asserted before, we could easily prove it. Not only is Christ worthily praised, and at least impliedly worshipped, in such hymns as 94, 99. 114, 143, but his Divinity is positively stated, here and there. Witness hymn 107, v. 3: "He rises and appears a God:" 157, v. 3: "The rising God forsakes the tomb:" 172, v. 1: "Your God and King adore."

The Atonement is indicated in hymns 119, 120, 144, and in lines like these:

"Eternal life to all mankind   Thou hast in Jesus given:"
"He died that we might live:"   "Thou hast redeemed our souls with blood."

The creed and life of Christianity are here; but less is made of them than might and ought to be ; and these most important points, though not ignored or denied, are, as Dr. Reynolds says, thrown into the background and the shade ; the compilers seem not to have emphasized these, though they believed them ; a horror of systematic divinity and of clear strong statement appears to have prevailed ; anything like technical terms and formulas were dreaded ; a broad church manual was seemingly designed, in which there should be nothing to offend professed believers of whatsoever type, and through which young people and outsiders might be mildly broken in to Christianity, by considerable exercise in natural religion. Thus the matters which all people who believe anything, are agreed upon, truths which Jews knew, and respectable heathen had some idea of, are here made prominent. General worship, the Divine Attributes, Providence, &c., are represented very fully. God in nature, in history, in our daily life, is set forth ; and the duties of gratitude, trust, and obedience, "our reasonable service," insisted on. Now all this is very well, and not to be despised. We are sometimes apt to forget or undervalue the light of Nature in the brighter blaze of Revelation ; whereas God is equally the Author of both, and intended both to be thankfully used by us. We cannot sing or preach exclusively about Jesus, the Atonement, and a living Faith, vastly important and edifying as these subjects are. Some of us, possibly, run to this extreme ; the New York book fell into the other. It is not easy to pardon the absence of "Rock of Ages," "There is a fountain," and "When I survey the wondrous cross ;" nor to be content that the person and work of Christ, in all their phases, should be represented by but eighty-one hymns, half of them very languid, dreary, and lifeless ; nor to sing at the Holy Communion, such as :

"Around the patriot's bust ye throng ;   Him ye exalt in swelling song." (Hymn 389.)

And yet this sample of sacred poesy is in the General Synod's book too !

As a natural result of the plan stated above, large prominence was given to the works, principles, and sentiments which were supposed to characterize the Christian. We might expect a humanistic tone here ; and a few of the pieces do savor more of the pride of nature than of the humility of Grace. Witness this astonishing production :

"The man whose firm and equal mind
To solid glory is inclined,
Determined will his path pursue,
And keep the God-like prize in view.
His calm, undaunted, manly breast,
Of virtue, honor, truth possest,
Will stem the torrent of the age,
And fearless tread this mortal stage."

The idea of singing that in church, as a hymn of praise to Almighty God, is somewhat stupendous. We are happy to be able, for once, to mention a fact which reflects credit on the General Synod's Collection. Strange as it may appear, this surprising effusion is not in it. A number more of these social and personal duty hymns do well enough to read at home, but are scarcely fit for the worship of the sanctuary. "If solid happiness we prize," (beginning in the original, "Dear Chloe, while the busy crowd;") is a famous and admirable moral poem, but not remarkably Christian ; and good Dr. Cotton, who wrote it, a pious man and a hymnist, had no idea of offering it to be sung in church. "Daughters of pity, tune the lay," is a singular beginning for a hymn ; and "absurd and vain attempt, to bind with iron chains the freeborn mind," might afford consolation to the persecuted British dissenters of old, but is scarcely appropriate in America, where nobody proposes to bind us.

It requires no vast stretch of magnanimity to make allowances for the faults of the New York Collection. Every age has its peculiar tone and temper, and exhibits its own phases of character and influence, in matters political, social, literary, religious, and what not. Half a century ago, English Hymnology was a comparatively recent, loose, and unfounded thing ; we have seen more than one decidedly orthodox and distinctively evangelical collection of that day, which yet contains matter as humanitarian in statement and spirit as

one can easily find. And if the book before us be not quite
so distinctively evangelical or decidedly orthodox as we
could wish, let us think of its Christian authors with something of that charity which we are taught to exercise toward
the heathen ; remembering that if we had been in their
place, under their surroundings, we might have done worse.
For it is more than doubtful whether their successors, in proportion to their lights, opportunities and convictions, have
done at all so well.

Supplement to New York Collection, 1834. 180 *Hymns.*

Of the Committee (appointed September, 1833,) who prepared this, Dr. Mayer was the Chairman ; and he, either
alone, or chiefly did the work. About half the hymns are
such as had either appeared, or become known since 1814,
being from Montgomery, Heber, Bowring. Kelly, the Spirit
of the Psalms (British), the American Episcopal Collection,
and similar, then recent, sources. Dr. Reynolds says, "there
is, perhaps, more unction and a higher tone of literary composition in these additional hymns," "but without making
any material change in the spirit" of the book. This is
hardly up to the truth. The *doctrine* of the volume may
not indeed be changed thereby, but its *spirit* is very considerably modified and improved. The new hymns, above mentioned, are, very many of them, high in devotional character. It is scarcely necessary to say that Montgomery, while
he belongs to, and leads the last or composite class of English
hymnology, was largely formed by, and deeply in sympathy
with, the new Wesleyan school ; or that positive orthodoxy
and warm feeling are essential characteristics of that school,
and of its true disciples. So much for the character of
a large proportion of the more modern among the
additional hymns, and of the older hymns thus added,
many are new-school in source and character. A few of
Charles Wesley's best are taken ; and Cowper, Newton,
Cennick, Williams, Seagrave, contribute noble Methodist
lyrics (so they may be called, since these men lived and
wrote in strong sympathy with the great Wesleyan revival),
which had been overlooked or rejected in 1814. A glance
at such hymns as 579, 581, 583, 584, 593, 601, 614, 616,
623, 629, 630, 631, 634, 635, 639, 688, 692, will show what
an advance has been gained in spirit, tone, temper, what enlarged scope of view and belief, what greater depth and
earnestness of Christian feeling, on the old collection. There

are, comparatively and positively, few hymns here of the
sort so numerous among the 520 of 1814; productions in
dull, decorous Long Metre, laboriously undoctrinal, and most
moderately devotional; verses such as Butcher, Jervis, Scott
and Needham, whole or half Arians, and exceedingly quiet
independents, used to write. One or two pieces, as 541, 543,
547, 552, celebrate the Redeemer somewhat unworthily,
considering the numbers of really fine Advent, Passion, and
Jesus hymns, which the language does and did then afford;
and as many, like 536, 537, 585, 607, moralize over providence, virtue, and such half-natural matters, in a tone that
reminds one of the old book, but these are the exceptions.
There is one effusion, however, to which we think we are justified in indulging a peculiar aversion: No. 594, headed
"Efficacy of Repentance." The first two verses are founded
on Isaiah 1 : 19, and promise the pardon of sin : and then
follows this surprising statement :

"By penitence and prayer,	*Bathed in the hallowed dews*
The wondrous change is wrought;	*Of deep compunction's tears,*
They soothe the pangs of dark de-	*The soul her health and strength re-*
spair,	*news,*
And heal the wounded thought,	*And meet for Heaven appears."*

Does it, indeed? Not much, in our opinion, or in that of
any New Testament writer with whom we are acquainted.
The man who wrote the above *meant* the heresy which it ex-
presses ; but it is hardly necessary to say, that neither Dr.
Mayer, nor any other, who is likely to have been engaged
with him on this Supplement, believed that sort of doctrine.
The thing must have been admitted by mere carelessness, the
compiler—as should not, but often does happen—not looking
below the surface, to discern the real character and latent
faults of the matter with which he had to deal.

Two hymns from the German are found in this supplement :
No. 582, being a fragment from John Wesley's rendering,
"Jesus, thy boundless love to me," of Gerhardt's famous
love-hymn : and 569, altered from part of Toplady's varia-
tion of J. C. Jacobi's version of *"O du allerduste Freude."*
Both fine lyrics.

The literary merit of this supplement is much above that
of the earlier part. A collection which, put together thirty
years ago, has three-fourths of its contents fully up to the
standard or average of respectable hymn books of this day,
and half of them worthy of retention by a severe and educa-

ted taste, deserves considerable praise. Taken all in all, it is a successful, creditable, and useful work ; and this, almost the only printed memorial which Dr. Mayer left, is not unworthy of his honored name, of his pure and lofty character, nor of his long, laborious, faithful, and believing life.

(*To be continued.*)

ARTICLE IV.

EXEMPLARY PIETY IN THE MINISTRY.*

By Rev. Milton Valentine, A. M., Reading, Pa.

The Address by Paul to Timothy, (1 Tim. 4 : 12,) indicates that he had been deeply impressed with the relations of the minister's own life to the proper accomplishment of his official work. He was convinced of the prime importance of *exemplary holiness*, in this sacred position. Possibly his mind reverted to the sad blight on religion in the case of the scribes and Pharisees, who, sitting in Moses' seat in the Jewish Church, "said, and did not." Perhaps the brief experience of the Christian Church had already developed this necessity. Probably it was plain on general principles, apart from experience,—flashing out before the mind as a self-evident truth. *Certain*, at any rate, is it, that he was led by the Holy Ghost, to give this direct and standing charge on the subject. Turning aside from the large field of doctrinal discussion in reference to the ministerial office, we wish to occupy our thoughts at this time with a more practical meditation on *the Duty of Exemplary Piety in the Ministry.*

It might seem superfluous to speak of this duty. All who are in the ministry, and all accepted candidates for it, are presumed fully to understand it. Doubtless they do. Not for "instruction," may it be needed, but for "admonition." It is profitable, often to renew our impression of its importance, and by fixing it afresh in our minds, quicken our endeavors after a purer blamelessness and perfection of charac-

*Delivered by appointment of the East Pennsylvania Synod at its last meeting, and published in the *Review* by the unanimous request of the Synod.

THE

EVANGELICAL

QUARTERLY REVIEW.

NO. LXII.

APRIL, 1865.

———◆———

ARTICLE IV.

LUTHERAN HYMNOLOGY.

By Rev. FREDERIC M. BIRD, A. M., Philadelphia, Pa.

IN the January number of the *Quarterly*, we gave such account as seemed fit of the various English hymnals prepared and published in the State or by the Synod of New York.

We are now to present such compilations as other ecclesiastical bodies, or individuals of our communion, have at any time put forth. And we shall do this as nearly in chronological order as the natural groupings and relationships of the books will permit.

Maryland Selection, 1822, 314 *Hymns*.

Probably not one of our readers will know, at first sight, what this heading means : and we doubt if ten of them have either seen or heard of the book until now. Its title, indeed, to a place in this article is questionable, for the word "Lutheran" is found neither within its covers nor on its back. But of that presently.

The title page reads: "The Pocket Selection of Hymns, for the use of Evangelical Churches, and Religious Assemblies, in the United States. Being a Collection from the Best Authors. First Edition. Frederick County, Md. Printed and Published by Matthias Bartgis, at Pleasant Dale Paper Mill, 1822." Overleaf is the Copyright, regularly taken out) and signed by "Philip Moore, Clerk of the District of Maryland." Then comes the preface, which we give entire, because it combines the virtue of brevity with a rare measure of bad grammar and impudent mendacity. (We give the *commas* verbatim ; and regret to state that a similar usage appears to be gaining ground among the printers of this day.) "The following Hymns, from various hymn-books, which are approved of by Protestants generally. Great care has been taken, to select such, as are practical. And, although this little volume has been compiled, for the use of families, private religious meetings, and Sunday Schools principally, yet several denominations using them during public worship, they may be of general utility to Christians.—It is unnecessary to add anything more, for a perusal of the hymns, will convince the attentive reader, that they coincide perfectly with the spirit of the Gospel." A more palpable collocation of lies we have never seen in print. This is the "First Edition;" how then could "several denominations" be already "using them," if by *them* is meant "this little volume"?—The cool assumption in the last sentence sounds greatly like the Unitarians of a former day, who were always insisting that their system was simple, pure, catholic Christianity, and that any believer, of whatever shade, must perforce be satisfied with what suited *them*. As for the hymns "coinciding perfectly with the spirit of the Gospel," their

prevailing tone is low Arian, and their general level very
flat, bare, and lifeless. And so far from being "selected
from various hymn-books," there is not a verse or a line in
this virtuous volume that is not taken, bodily and literally,
from the New York book of 1814. The whole thing is a
stupendous piece of literary piracy. Nothing is changed except the *order* of the hymns, and that only enough to thinly
cloak the cheat. The subjects (of which there is no separate
index) runs thus: I. Attributes of God, hymn 1; II
Works and Providence of God, 18; III. The Scripture, 32;
IV. Praise and Thanksgiving, 41; V. Mission and Nativity
of Christ, 51; VI. Office and Mediation of Christ, 56;
VII. Example of Christ, 66; VIII. Suffering and Death
of Christ, 70; IX. Resurrection of Christ, 81; X. Holy
Spirit, 87; XI. Prayer, 96; XII. Danger and Misery of
Sin, 105; XIII. Conversion, 115; XIV. The Christian
Character, 124; XV. Joy and Felicity of True Christians,
134; XVI. Faith and Duties of Piety, 144; XVII. Per-
sonal and Social Duties, 164; XVIII. Public Worship, 189;
XIX. Baptism, 207; XX. Lord's Supper, 210; XXI.
Morning, 220; XXII. Evening, 226; XXIII. New Year,
229; XXIV. National Blessings and Afflictions, 232;
XXV. For a Congregation, 243; XXVI. Sickness and Re-
covery, 248; XXVII. Troubles of Life, 255; XXVIII.
For the Young and Old, 265; XXIX. Death, 271; XXX.
Resurrection, 295; XXXI. Judgment and End of the
World, 298; XXXII. Heaven, 304. This arrangement, it
will be seen, is almost identical with that of the New York
Collection: in several instances Heads are transposed: in one
or two they are lumped together; the Church is left out in
the cold, and the word Repentance is omitted: these, with a
few verbal alterations, make the whole difference. The same
hymns in each book stand under the same subject, with no
other change than may be produced by typographical errors.
Thus No. 1 in this Maryland affair is No. 32 in the New
York book; 2 corresponds to 33, &c.

It is possible, and easy, to make a very dull and tame book
from the New York one. The unknown and unhonored
patcher-up of this thing before us seems to have aimed at
this laudable result; he certainly attained it. The Trochaic
and other Peculiar Measures, which give variety and life to a
hymn-book, are carefully excluded from this: it contains
nothing but L. M., C. M., S. M. and one sample of L. M. C.
lines. The few hymns like "One there is above all others,"

"Join all the glorious names," "Now begin the heavenly theme," "Christ the Lord is risen to-day," which form the chief redeeming feature of the collection of 1814, find no place here. Thus in doctrine, devotion, and poetry, it sinks a grade or two below its parent. A thing at once stolen and spoiled is detestable and unpardonable, before gods and men.

One curious feature remains to be noticed. *Six* hymns, as arranged here, are *double*; that is, two lyrics, successive or not, in the New York book will be joined under one number in this, without regard to their sense or spirit, beginning or end. Thus No. 262 begins with No. 466 in New York: "Weary of these low scenes of night," which rhymes by alternate lines; and at verse 5 takes up No. 468 of New York, a hymn of very different strain, rhyming by couplets, "My God, my hope! if Thou art mine." Thus the 314 hymns of this piratical volume correspond to 320 of the 520 in the New York collection.

We know nothing about the origin or history of this book; who got it up, where and how it was used, whether its shameless fraud was ever exposed, whether a second edition was ever printed, or anything more than appears from the book itself. We have seen and heard of but two copies, which are identical; one belonging to the writer, the other in the collection of that veteran hymnologist, David Creamer, Esq., of Baltimore. The book occupies 256 pages, is half an inch shorter than the recent editions of the New York collection, and about half as thick: it is printed on coarse dark paper, not saying much for the merits of "Pleasant Dale Paper Mills," but suggestive in our day, of Dixie: and is neatly bound in boards and half sheep, labelled simply "Hymns." And so ends our account, perhaps too lengthy, of a production only valuable as presenting probably the most remarkable mixture extant of doctrinal negativeness, devotional deadness, and moral dishonesty. May we never have such another.

Tennessee Hymn Book.   First Edition, 1815–16.

Our efforts to beg, buy, or borrow a copy of this scarce volume have been in vain; and we are not disposed to illuminate the Church with a minute account of what we have never seen. These facts appear; that it was prepared by Rev. Paul Henkel, and that many, probably the large majority, of its contents were from his own pen. We fancy that the following criticism, passed by an eminent English

Authority, Dr. Neale of Sackville College, on one of the earliest Christian poems, the *Instructiones* of Commodianus, would apply here: "Nothing, in the way of poetry, can be more utterly worthless; but there are a few allusions which render it valuable to the Christian antiquary, and a vein of pious simplicity pervades the whole."

Tennessee Hymn Book. Second Edition, 1838, 679 *Hymns.*

We have never seen this Second Edition; but the third, 1850, is before us, with a Preface dated 1838. The two were identical, except five hymns added, and "a few orthographical changes," in the later, and on the basis of this general identity between the two, we shall proceed to notice the book, as if it were bodily, as it is substantially before us.

The title was, we suppose, mainly the same with that of the subsequent editions, which we give below. The Preface, which is signed "AMBROSE HENKEL, *Newmarket, Shenandoah Co. Va., August 15th,* 1838," gives such information as we have concerning the relation of this to the old edition. "This work is not an entire new and independent publication; but * * the principal matter of its contents has been in reputable demand for a considerable length of time in the Church; contained in the hymn book published in the years of 1815 and 16, compiled by my father, the late Rev. Paul Henkel, entitled "CHURCH HYMN BOOK," etc.; which work contains a considerable portion of hymns composed by the deceased himself; and marked thus ‡ throughout the work. As its contents are purely evangelical, and as the hymns apportioned to the GOSPELS and EPISTLES were much admired for their simplicity and strict accordance with their respective texts, connected with many other desirable qualities, it gained an extensive circulation. But, whatever encomiums that work deserves, it is now unobtainable: that edition being totally consumed by its many and extensive sales. It was therefore resolved by the Evangelical Lutheran Tennessee Synod, to devolve it upon me to make the present publication. This, though it varies in some respects from that work, is founded upon the same basis, and comprises essentially the same matter. Many additional hymns are selected from other authors: so that the attentive reader will now find two or more hymns for every text throughout the ecclesiastical year. He will also perceive, that this edition contains hymns on occasions which the former editions did not comprise.

Hymns not so well approved, were set aside, and others considered preferable, were substituted. Those that were deficient in point of language or in grammatical construction, are corrected. Watts' psalms are not retained entire and in the same order :" etc.

The Table of Contents occupies above three pages. Public Worship has hymns 1 to 16; For the Gospels and Epistles (separately indicated as far as Trinity Sunday,) 17 to 308, nearly half the volume; The Word of God, 309; Being and Perfection of God, 317; Works of God, 329; Providence of God, 337; Praise to God, 344; The Trinity, 356; Christ, 359; Holy Spirit, 387; The Law of God, 391; Fall and Depravity of Man, 398; The Gospel or Salvation through Jesus Christ, 403: Faith, 413; Repentance, 422; Justification, 431; Sanctification, 436; Prayer, 441; Christian Experience, 448; Baptism, 471; Catechising, 484; Confirmation, 496; Confession of Sin, 499; The Lord's Supper, 503; Ordination, 517; Dedicating of a Church, 523; Synod, 528; Table Hymns, 536; Morning Hymns, 543; Evening Hymns, 555; Sickness, 568; Death, 588; Resurrection, 308; General Judgment, 612; Heaven and Future Happiness, 618; Hell and Future Punishment, 625; Angels, 628; Civil Government, 631; Journeying Hymns, 645; Afflictions, 650; The Seasons, 658; The Stages of Life, 666; Doxologies, 671 to 679. Under some of these heads are minute and curious subdivisions; thus under "Civil Goverment," "For those who are imprisoned, For those who are to be executed, An officer or soldier leaving home, For an officer in camp, For a soldier in camp, Thanksgiving for a safe return from camp." The head "Table Hymns," is noticeable. The "vein of pious simplicity" is apparent in these.

For the authorship, Paul Henkel appears to contribute 302, seven are signed D. H., three S. A. H., and one C. H. One or two anonymous pieces may also be original. The rest are drawn from common sources : the compiler seeming to have especially possessed and used a copy of Watts, of Nettleton's Village Hymns, and of Rippon's Collection. Not very Churchly or Lutheran sources, but as good no doubt as were within his reach. Dr. Watts gives 161 hymns, C. Wesley 25, Doddridge 25, Steele 15, Newton 11, Beddome 8, Cowper 7, S. Stennet 7, Tate and Brady 5, Simon Brown 4, Hart, Fawcett, Collyer, Hyde, each 3, Addison, Cennick, Medley, Toplady, Kelly, Gibbons, Needham, each 2, while

the rest are various or anonymous. (This is our own computation; the authors of the originals only are indicated.)

As to the character and merits of the book, perhaps the
less we say the better. It never was used, we imagine, outside the narrow limits of the body for which it was prepared;
nor did it ever exert the least perceptible influence on any
other book or body: hence there is no occasion for such
close and full criticism as it is our duty to employ with hymnals which have been, are, or might be recognized and used
in any sense by the Church at large. The original author
of the Tennessee book was eminent for his ardent, active,
and self-denying love to the Church of his fathers. With
every disposition to appreciate his motives and look kindly
on his work, it is not possible to regard the latter as in any
sense a success. It might meet the wants of a small, isolated, and somewhat narrow communion, with little culture and
no æsthetic requirement, but it could not possibly do more.
James Montgomery and Josiah Conder have published hymn
books, with a large proportion (though by no means so large
as Mr. Henkel's) of their own matter; but even that hardly
succeeded; and Mr. Henkel was not Conder or Montgomery.
His productions might possibly edify a converted backwoods-
man or a slave of the Uncle Tom type,—though we think
this would be more readily done by the Campmeeting lyrics
to which Hardshell Baptists and sometimes Methodists greatly do incline,—but they never could come into anything like
recognized use, among civilized people, in this nineteenth
century. Nor are the selections of the Tennessee book at
all the best which the language affords. The fact is, true
churchliness is a thing graceful, cultivated, liberal, large, enlightened, attractive; and, not as too many suppose, a
narrow, old-timey thing of fossils and forms. The misery
and mischief has been, that those who had the truth have
so seldom been able to represent it worthily. The few English hymnals which have proceeded from distinctively
churchly portions of our communion in America are but
poorly adapted to serve the cause which created them, or to
illustrate and extend the faith in which they were put forth.
If the Lutheran Church is ever to be more nearly united
than now, in sound belief and just practice, one essential
means to that great end must be a Hymnal vastly better, in
matter, style and spirit, than anything we have had yet.

The principle of arranging hymns for the successive Sun-
days of the whole Christian Year, on which so large a part

of the book before us is constructed, has been tried several times, usually within the Church of England, and never with success. Such a division, if standard hymns are used, must be too arbitrary to be reasonable or convenient; and hymns made to order are vastly worse than none at all. The whole plan savors too much of foregoing the liberty of the spirit, and submitting to the bondage of the letter. Henkel's verses on the Gospels and Epistles are mostly mere hortatory or didactic paraphrases, with almost nothing lyrical, still less hymnic, about them, and usually on a dead level. One sample is enough. For Septuagesima, Matt. 20: 1—6.

First verse:

In parables the Lord doth show How to perform their duty well,
What gospel ministers must do— We find here in this parable.

Tenth and last verse:

They teach, admonish, and reprove, They act with fervency and zeal,
And all they do is out of love: And God rewards their labors well.

The practice of singing that sort of stuff Sunday after Sunday, under pretence of praising God, we should consider decidedly insane, and somewhat impious. However, that is the Tennessee Synod's affair, not ours. But some of his pieces are better than this. Especially No. 35, which is from a fine Advent Hymn of Gerhardt:

"Immanuel; we sing thy praise, We worship Thee with one accord,
Thou Prince of life! Thou Spring Thou virgin's Son! Thou Lord of
    of grace!   lords!

It is a pity that nothing marks such hymns as Mr. Henkel may have translated from the German. There may be a number, (though hardly a *large* number:) but we have recognized only one or two, and to identify others would require more time and trouble than the book deserves.

Tennessee Hymn Book.   Third Edition.   1850.

Contains *four* additional hymns, numbered 41 *A*, 151 *A*, 354 *A*, 627 *A*, & 520 *A*. The first four have the initials J. S., and are translations from the German; one of them a rendering of Luther's Christmas carol, another of "Jesus meine Zuversicht." They are considerably better than Mr. Henkel's originals, and about as good as the translated hymns in the General Synod's Collection. The other has Mr. Henkel's mark. We promised above to give the Title Page:

"Church Hymn Book : consisting of Hymns and Psalms, original and selected ; adapted to Public Worship, and many other occasions. By the Rev. Paul Henkel. Published by order of the Evangelical Lutheran Tennessee Synod. Third Edition Enlarged and Improved. Newmarket: Solomon D. Henkel & Brothers—Joseph Fink & Sons, Mountain Valley, near Harrisonburg, Va., Printers & Binders. 1850." 24mo. pp. XIV, 546.

Tennessee Hymn Book. Fourth Edition. 1857.

Differs from the last only in having 46 new hymns scattered through the book, and marked *A. B. C.*, &c., leaving the numbers of the old hymns untouched. The hymns here added are mostly well known and respectable, and are an improvement to the book. 402 *A*, is by Rev. M. Loy, and is taken from the Ohio book. Of the remaining 45, nine are from Watts, four each from Steele and Newton, and the rest from single or unknown authors. This edition has 576 pages, and, like its predecessors, is about equal in size to the 24mo issue of the General Synod.

General Synod's Book. Old Edition, 1828, 766 *Hymns.*

We shall notice this work under its own head no further than as it differs from the present Edition ; proposing to extend and unite our remarks upon that as a whole. The Title and Preface are the same, except that the latter in the old book, contains this paragraph, afterward omitted : "As the New York Hymn Book is in the possession of many of our churches, it was thought proper to add to all the hymns taken from it the number which they bear in that collection : and as the number of such hymns in all the principal divisions of that book is very considerable, it will be found that both books can be used together without inconvenience." And after the signatures and date, comes a certificate from the President and Secretary of the General Synod, D. Kurtz, D. D., and D. F. Schaeffer, "that this Hymn Book is published under the sanction of the General Synod of the Ev. Lutheran Church in the U. S., and in conformity to the resolution of said body, passed October the 27th, 1827." The table of Contents is substantially the same, except that there are many subdivisions here, occupying four full pages. Thus "XV. Christian Experience" contains "1. The Convert entertaining a hope of pardon ; and the happiness of the Christian. 2. Communion with Christ and love to Him.. 3. Doubts and fears. 4. Spiritual Declension. 5. Backslider returning. 6. Sanctification and Christian graces. 7. The Christian life figuratively described as Taking up the Cross, A Pilgrimage, A Voyage, Scene of troubles, A Warfare, A Desert. 8. Christian assurance and confidence in God. 9. Christian in the prospect of death." Foolish as much of this is, it is probably better than to have six or eight score of lyrics lumped together,—as is done in the present General Synod's book,—under one sweeping title which may mean anything, everything, or nothing, and without the slightest attempt to classify or divide.

We notice 44 hymns in this book, and there may be several more, which were omitted when the book was revised. Most of them, we can cheerfully say, were admirably adapted to be thrown away, and exceedingly useless for any other purpose. Among them (No. 726) is a pleasing product of Dr. Watts' genius, devoted apparently to the celebration of "abominable fiends," and beginning

"My thoughts on awful subject roll,   Damnation and the dead (!)"

And another elegant effusion (411), by the same respected but not infallible writer :

'My heart, how dreadful hard it is !   Heavy and cold within my breast,
How heavy here it lies !   Just like a rock of ice !"

No. 220, by Henry Kirke White, has often drawn amazed and bewildered attention. Pretty enough as a poem, it is a sample of the sublime absurdity of putting a thing into a hymn book simply because its author was a good man, and wrote some other things, which *are* hymns.

"What is this passing scene ?   And all things fade away :
  A peevish April day :   Man (soon discussed)
A little sun, a little rain,   Yields up his trust,
And then night sweeps along the   And all his hopes and fears lie with
    plain,   him in the dust !"

And so on. We do not see why the compilers did not also insert "Lilly Dale" and "Auld Robin Gray," which are quite as pathetic, nearly as sacred, and about as hymnic in character.

But we have more serious fault to find with No. 184 and 356. It was bad enough for Charles Wesley to write these; it is infinitely worse for members of a Church which holds the truth, and has no occasion or temptation to resort to such forms of error, to drag them into use. In matter, spirit, style, doctrine, tone, tendency, they are the most distinctively and objectionably methodistic poems which the Methodist poet ever penned. The first purports to be a hymn of invitation, and offers certain inducements, Christ's "proffered benefits," "the plenitude of gospel grace," which are supposed to be as follows:

2. "A pardon written with his blood,
   The favor and the peace of God;
   The seeing eye, the feeling sense,
   The trembling joys of penitence:

4. The guiltless shame, the sweet distress,
   The unutterable tenderness:
   The genuine, meek humility;
   The wonder, "Why such love to me?"

3. The godly fear, the pleasing smart,
   The meltings of a broken heart:
   The tears that tell your sins forgiven;
   The sighs that waft your souls to heaven;

5. The o'erwhelming power of saving grace
   The sight that veils the seraph's face,
   The speechless awe that dares not more,
   And all the silent heaven of love!"

These rhapsodies and ecstasies, these meltings and tremblings, these unutterable tendernesses and sweet distresses, may be very delightful; but as for there being anything specially sacred or divine about them, *that* idea is exploded; or, at least, ought to be. The truth is with the churchly writer:

"Faith's meanest *deed* more favor bears,
   Where heart and wills are weighed!

Than brightest transports, choicest prayers,
   That bloom their hour and fade.

Nor is this sort of thing objectionable only on theoretic grounds, as a matter of abstract truth or error. When we are taught, as in the second verse quoted, that tears and sighs are means of grace, that our private emotional gymnastics may take the place of, or coöperate with, the eternal merits and untold agonies of our blessed Lord,—then the way is open before us to the worst forms of fanaticism, and to any degree of Pharisaic self-delusion. We may not get there indeed; we may not go so far; but the fault is not with the road, nor with those who lead us on it.—The other hymn is worse yet, if possible, being a cool, explicit, straightforward statement of that pernicious heresy, the doctrine, as it has fitly enough been called, of "Justification by Sensation." It tells its own story:

"How can a sinner know
  His sins on earth forgiven?
How can my gracious Saviour show
  My name inscribed in heaven?

What we have *felt* and *seen*
  With confidence we tell;
And publish to the sons of men
  The signs infallible.

We who in Christ believe
  That he for us hath died,
We all his unknown peace receive,
  And feel his blood applied!

Exults our rising soul,
  Delivered of her load,
And *swells unutterably full*
  Of glory and of God."

We opine that a frail human heart—especially if it be so "unutterably full"—is more likely to "swell" with pride and vain self-conceit, than with the fruit of the Spirit, which among other things is gentleness, meekness, temperance; and that a man who erects his hope on the "infallible" basis of fluctuating moods and sensations, is likely to find it a house built upon the sand. Charles Wesley, and some of his converts, were men of such earnest faith and exalted holiness, that they might be able to hold, in theory, a vital and pestilent error, without having the spiritual life poisoned or undermined thereby; but to teach the masses that their feelings are infallible is a most dangerous experiment, and liable to ruin as many souls as the truth, which may be mixed up with such false teaching, will save. Our Methodist brethren have a right to believe and sing what they like; but we do object to anybody's palming off this sort of heresy upon us, in an official book of the Churh, as Lutheran doctrine. We ought perhaps to say, that the first of these two hymns has found its way into one Episcopal collection, (very low Church of course,) and into another which is nominally Arian. But the fact that others have committed an offence does not justify us in committing it too.

We should be guilty of a sad sin of omission if we did not notice what is in some respects the most astounding production we know in this—or any other—book: No. 463. We never saw it elsewhere, and know not who wrote it; probably some otherwise mute, and altogether inglorious, Milton. By way of guide to the blind, and help towards the otherwise unfathomable meaning, it has the heading, "Conflict between sin and holiness:"

"When heaven does grant at certain times,
Amidst a pow'rful gale,
Sweet liberty to moan my crimes,
And wand'rings to bewail—

Then do I dream my sinful brood
Is drown'd in the wide main
Of crystal tears a crimson blood,
And ne'er will live again."

The usual effect of this lyric upon our faculties is speechless amazement and admiration; but we will endeavor to throw off the spell, and analyze the teachings of these "powerful" verses. In the first place we find that Repentance is a pleasing and luxurious exercise; "*sweet* liberty." Secondly, that this attractive indulgence is not always to be had: you cannot repent when you will, but only "at certain times." Thirdly, the surroundings must be favorable; it must be "amidst a powerful gale." If the weather be calm, you can neither do the works, nor enjoy the delightful sensations, which belong to true penitence. Such is the doxy of the first verse. Now when these necessary elements are all provided,—when Heaven has granted the certain times, the powerful gale, and the sweet liberty,—what next? What comes of such grand preparation? Then the narrator,—we know not whether to call him subject, patient, or medium,—*dreams.* And what does he dream? That his sins are a litter, cruelly doomed, "ah, alas!" to a watery grave, and actually enduring that untimely and unmerited extinction. (It is not quite a watery grave either; his metaphor is mixed a little; but none the worse for that.) And having thus effectually "drowned" them in the first three-quarters of his second verse, the poet condescends to the requirements of metre, and obligingly informs us, in the remaining line, that they "ne'er will live again." Having exhausted himself by this surprising figure of speech, he after this says what he has to say—such as it is—in plain language.

"I get my foes beneath my feet,
I bruise the serpent's head;
I hope the victory is complete,
And all my lusts are dead.

But ah, alas! th' ensuing hour
My passions rise and swell;
They rage and reinforce their pow'r
With new recruits from hell."

Of course they do. What else can be expected, when a man puts his sensations on the throne of God, and looks to frames and feelings for Justification and Sanctification, instead of the blessed Trinity? And this is the sort of religion which some would substitute for the faith of the Confessions and of the Fathers! We fancy that the whole system, in its practical workings, is apt to end, as this sample of a spiritual song so fitly does, "with new recruits from hell." From such heresy, whether sung, prayed, preached, or published, may the Lord deliver his Church.

General Synod's Enlarged Edition, 1841, 965 *Hymns*.

If any one wishes to know who was responsible for this, we suppose he can ascertain from the Minutes of the General Synod. It was the Hymn Book Committee: and of that Committee Dr. Schmucker's name appears as Chairman. Beyond this we are in blissful and contented ignorance. For when we cannot praise, and must not be silent, we gladly escape alike the temptation and the appearance of being personal. Very good men sometimes do very bad deeds: our business is with the deeds, not the men.

Sundry minor improvements were here made in the old book, and two hymns, Nos. 220 and 251, were displaced by others. The first of these is "What is this passing scene?" above referred to: it is here substituted by Watts' tame and characterless paraphrase of part of the 49th Psalm. The other is a lamentation of good Joseph Hart, of more reputation than merit; it had been repeated in No. 253, and here yields to a poem on the same subject, but in vastly different style. It would have been as well if the Editors had used their power in omitting a few more, like 749, and 341.

"I'm bound for New Jerusalem;"	* * * * *
"Lord, and am I yet alive,	Tell it unto sinners, tell,
Not in torrents, not in hell !	I am, I am out of hell!"
* * * * *	

But such cruel mutilations of the book's truth and beauty were by no means part of their plan. And so all that we have here to comment on is the Appendix of 199 hymns.

It is difficult to understand the principle on which this Selection was made. The lowest taste and judgment seem to prevail; a reckless inconsistency, in doctrine, temper, style, and spirit, runs riot: Low Church and Broad Church, are mixed into an agreeable compound, presenting some of the worst qualities of both, with not much of the redeeming features of either. Such genuine hymns as Alexander's rendering of "O Haupt voll blut und wunden" and Sir Robert Grant's "solemn Litany" are put in company with rollicking camp-meeting melodies: from one page we sing: "All hail the power of Jesus' name," and on the next we are invited to join in this :

'"Saw ye my Saviour—Saw ye my Saviour—Saw ye my Saviour and God?"

The original of which is, we think, better of its kind, and certainly more consistent with its subject, than the above parody :

"Saw ye my wee thing?   Saw ye my ain thing?
Saw ye my true love down on yon lea?"

There are a number of lyrics addressed to "Wandering pilgrims, mourning Christians,

Weak and tempted lambs of Christ."

And one considerately inquires :

"Mourner is thy case distressing?"

Well might the Ohio compilers (1845) complain of "the strange bias of many hymns in the book." Several more, though of a higher order, are hardly more adapted to the purposes of public worship, being mere sentimental songs on sacred subjects.   Thus 804, "O turn ye, O turn ye, for why will ye die?" and 803,

"When the harvest is past, and the   When the beams cease to break of
    summer is gone,   the sweet Sabbath morn,
And sermons and prayers shall   And Jesus invites thee no more,"
    be o'er ;   &c.

This latter is a very favorable sample.   However pretty these may be, and however occasionally impressive, they ought not to be sung in Church.   The sermon may exhort men as much as it pleases ; the hymns should be allowed to praise God.

The singular quantity and quality of these versified exhortations are not the only indication of the loose taste which marks this Appendix.   At its very beginning we stumble over three Old Testament tales, forced into metre by good John Newton ; things which were doubtless edifying enough for the Olney cottagers to read, but are by no means fit for us to sing ; Nos. 768—790.   Further on (845,) is a familiar piece of Toplady's, but familiar only in Calvinistic books ; a piece which has for its subject, basis, and sole inspiration, the predestinarian doctrine of Perseverance ; a piece headed, in the author's works, "Full Assurance," and insisting on that "assurance" in a manner not repugnant to the instincts, intellect and conscience of a non-Calvinist, and greatly adapted, as non-Calvinists would be apt to think, to encourage the fanaticism, Pharasaism, and Antinomianism which naturally grow under the wing of such a creed as Toplady's. Here is the last half verse :

"Yes ! I to the end shall endure,   More happy, but *not more secure,*
  As sure as the earnest is given ;   *The glorified spirits in heaven.*"

To put *that* in the official hymn book of a Church which never held the doctrines of Assurance and Perseverance, which always admitted the possibility of Falling from Grace, requires catholicity of spirit indeed.   Whether the compilers of this Appendix did not know what was Lutheran doctrine, did not care whether what they put in agreed with Lutheran doctrine or not, or did not look beyond the first line of the hymns which they inserted, is an open question.

One more quotation will conclude our disagreeable task of pointing out the gross faults in a compilation that has few features which are not faults.   No. 948 is that horrible product of a diseased imagination or depraved conscience, which is unfortunately too well known in America.   The bare idea of anybody singing it, under whatever circumstances, is shocking ; it would be intolerable, we should think, amidst the "raving profanity" of the wildest camp-meeting ; and the sin of printing it in a Church hymn book is not easily to be pardoned.   The few who may happily not know it can fancy its dreadful repetitions from a single verse :

"O ! there will be mourning   *Friends and kindred there will part,*
  Before the judgment seat ;   *Will part to meet no more !*
When this world is burning   *Wrath will sink the rebel's heart,*
  Beneath Jehovah's feet !   *While saints on high adore !*"

This gloating over the horrors of eternity, and making out that the purified spirits of the redeemed will rejoice to see their children, husbands, brothers sink into the firey lake, is the sort of religion that has made infidels by the thousand.

Of the 199 hymns in this Appendix, only 99 were thought fit to be retained, at the subsequent revision.   If we have said much about what is no longer in existence, it is because the Past goes far to form the Present.   During eleven years this book was used by most of our English churches ; and in that time what vast harm it may and must have done !

Hoffman's Hymns, 1838, 247 *H.*

The only book of the kind, so far as we know, that our communion has ever produced. The title page tells its own story : "Evangelical Hymns : Original and selected : Designed for the use of Families and Private Circles ; for Social Prayer-Meetings, Seasons of Revival, or other Occasions of Special Interest. By Rev. J. N. Hoffman. 'I will sing of Mercy and Judgment.' Chambersburg, Pa. Published by W. O. Hickok. 1838." 24mo, 156 pages. The Preface says the book is meant to supply the felt want of a Collection "adapted especially to the prevalence of Revivals, which are so characteristic of the present age. * * The work contains a number of Hymns which have been composed since most Books, now used by the Church, were published. * * Care has been taken to give the work a strictly devotional character, and to adapt it to the various exigencies of the awakened and enquiring. No hymns contained in the Lutheran Hymn Book now in use, have been admitted into this Collection, while many on those subjects on which the former is not sufficiently full, have been added." From these statements it will be seen that the plan and tendency of the book is, as nearly everything at that day was, distinctively new-measure : yet certain ordinances peculiar to our Church are worthily emphasized, as will appear from the order of contents. Being, and Attributes, and Word of God, Hymn 1: Christ, 8: Holy Spirit, 30: Worship, 41: Fall and Human Depravity, 56: Revivals, 61: Penitential, 74: Expostulating, 89: Inviting, 96: Christian Experience, 116: Praise, 148: Church and Kingdom of Christ, 155: Catechetical, 170: Confirmation, 183: Missionary, 192: Death and Judgment, 203: Heaven, 215: Miscellaneous, 221: Dismission, 231: Doxologies, 234–247. The Catechetical and Confirmation hymns are not of any great merit, but their number shows more attention to one of our most important points of practice than the general tenor of the book would have warranted us in expecting. This book appeared three years before the General Synod's Appendix, and some of its hymns were afterwards transferred to that. We find "O sacred Head" here, No. 27, in the same abridged reading —a very good one—which is kept in the General Synod. As to the "Original Hymns," we suppose them to be three marked H. M., one H.—and perhaps two which we do not otherwise know, but possessing considerable force, by "Mrs.

McCartee." Of these one or two were reprinted in the subsequent Appendix to General Synod. "Mourner, is thy case distressing," is, we suppose, by Mr. Hoffman: "Quench not the Spirit of the Lord," which is in the present General Synod's Collection—at least in some copies—insanely and slanderously ascribed to Charles Wesley, is credited in Hoffman to "M. S.," but is by Thomas Hastings.

The book does not call for any special criticism. Watts gives 34 hymns, C. Wesley 11; we have not taken the trouble to count the rest. The great majority of the contents are not worth preserving; but hardly any of them sink so low as those we have quoted, and a number more, in the General Synod's Appendix of 1841. A spirit of sincere and earnest piety pervades the volume; and it is a good enough compilation for the purpose.

Dr. Krauth's S. S. Hymns, 1838. 217 : 10 H.

The first English Lutheran Sunday School Hymn Book: its author was then pastor of St. Matthew's Church, Philadelphia. Title: "Hymns, Selected and Arranged for Sunday Schools, of the Evangelical Lutheran Church, and adapted to Sunday Schools in general. Philadelphia: William Brown, Printer, 1838." 32mo., 181 pages of hymns, and ten of First lines. Contents: I. Hymns on God and his works, 1. II. The Doctrines of Christianity. a. The source of them, 3. b. What God is and does, 5. c. Angels, 9. d. Jesus Christ, and the Holy Spirit, 10. III. The means of Grace, 21. IV. The Duties of human beings and the Christian Character, 27. V. Death, Resurrection Judgment, Eternity, 78. VI. Miscellaneous, a. Festivals and Anniversaries, 108; b. Diffusion of Religion, 125; c. Seasons, 129; d. For teachers at their meetings, 135; e. Special hymns for children, 162; f. Morning and Evening, 201; g. Parting and Dismission, 206; h. Doxologies, 212–217. Additional, 1–10.

Most of the contents are of the familiar sort, taken from the large books; comparatively few are distinctively children's hymns. Two are noticeable; one a Christmas hymn, No. 109, "Glory to God! the holy angels cry:" the other Moravian, from the Countess Zinzendorf. Its force and quaintness, standing solitary among two hundred English lyrics, strike one:

"When I visit Jesus' grave in spirit,
  It is never done in vain ;
Since 'tis only from his death and
  merit
  I can life and strength obtain.

Jesus' cross, his last hours in his
  passion,
Jesus' body and his blood,
Jesus' stripes, his wounds and ex-
  piration
Shall remain my highest good."

Rough that is, and unsingable, of course; but with more matter in it,—more doctrine, life. and solid truth and meaning—than twenty ordinary English hymns. The German language is the great fount of sacred song; and if our fathers, thirty, fifty years ago, had had a few dozen respectable translations from it and been willing to use them, the Church in America would be in better condition now.

Dr. Passavant's S. S. Hymns, 1843, 304 H.

"Hymns: Selected and Original, for Sunday Schools, of the Evangelical Lutheran Church; with a Supplement containing Hymns for the use of Infant Schools. Baltimore: Published by T. Newton Kurtz, No. 151 Pratt street." 32mo., pp. 256, xiv. Preface dated "Baltimore, Md., Aug. 28, 1843." This is much like the preceding, on which it is more or less based, and which it superseded. Having no particular character of any sort, there is not much to be said about it. But we have one idea (not original) to ventilate, which applies not only to this, but to most Sunday School Hymn Books, past and present, used by us or by other bodies. These books seem to forget that our Saviour took little children in his arms and blessed them ; that he declared the kingdom to be of such ; that he ordained the sacrament of baptism, whereby they become members of his Church, and receive the seed of regeneration. All this is ignored, and the Christian infant put on the same footing with men born, bred, and hardened in unresisted and unpardoned sin. He is prayed for, and taught to pray himself, as if he were a thief or murderer; dogmas of a perverse theology, which neither his head nor heart can take hold of, are piled around and above him, a wall sufficient to shut out the kindly light of heaven: hell-fire and lectures on innate depravity are flung in his face ; he is howled at, and groaned over: and the poor baptized innocent is taught to expect as necessary such a change as the persecutor Saul, or the profligate tinker Thomas Olivers, had to endure : to believe that God's good Spirit must come by abnormal spasms and agonies, when all the time he is trying to renew the soul—if men would but coöperate with him, or else let his work alone—by a gradual, gentle, imperceptible, but incessant process, from the earliest hours of life. Unfortunately both Dr. Watts and Charles Wesley held very erroneous views with regard to these matters; and the mass of inferior hymnists followed in their wake. Now we may preach the truth in vain, so long as we *sing* heresy: and with our hymn books, for children as well as adults, are made to conform to the Church's faith, we shall never have that peace which can only come after purity. The book before us (Dr. Passavant would do very differently now) is not worse than most, not so bad as many; but how inappropriate, for the distinctive use of children, are such hymns as these: "Child of sin and sorrow," "O that my load of sin were gone!" "Come, trembling sinner:" "Stay, thou insulted Spirit, stay:" "Where shall a guilty child retire:" "Lamb of God, for sinners slain:" "Let the world their virtue boast:" "Hell! 'tis a word of dreadful sound:" (Nos. 90, 100, 101, 104, 108, 110, 121, 139.)—How gross is this (93), if Dr. Watts did write it:

"What if the Lord grow wroth, and swear,
While I refuse to read and pray,
That He'll refuse to lend an ear,
To all my groans another day!

'Tis dangerous to provoke our God
His power and vengeance none can tell;
One stroke of his almighty rod
Shall send young sinners quick to hell."

Few things can be more insulting to the Lord and injurious to the child,—more sure to alienate affection and plant distrust, to undo all the effects of Holy Baptism and christian nurture—than this. The child, if he have a fair share of mind and spirit, will unconsciously rebel against such a God and such a government as this. The divinest things within him, his yet unperverted conscience, his tender heart, his native sense of fitness and right, cry out against such monstrous fictions, and refuse to own the tyrannous rule of brute force and coward fear. We have borne the incubus of these Puritan errors long enough: it is time the Church arose, in the sublime simplicity of her own pure faith, to give her children bread instead of stones, meat in place of poison.

Of course everything in the book is not bad; there are some lyrics of genuine simplicity and tenderness, well fitted to their work, as "When little Samuel woke," and "Gentle Jesus, meek and mild." But that there should be *any* such as we have indicated, is altogether wrong. If any one thinks we have said too much, or said it unnecessarily, we would remind him that the evil has not been abated; that the body of this book is still published by Mr. Kurtz, and used in many nominally Lutheran Sunday Schools. We are sorry for it.

Of the literary character of this work we have no need to speak. But here is its "Index of General Titles:" Character, Works, and Providence of God, *Page* 5; The Scriptures, 18; Prayer, 24; Praise, 36; Sunday School and Public Worship, 47; Early Piety, 68; Penitential, 84; Redemption through Jesus Christ, 97; Death, Judgment, Heaven and Hell, 107; Various Occasions and Subjects, (here come what there is of the Festivals) 119; Teachers' Meetings and Monthly Concerts, 160; Missionary, 182; Anniversary Occasions, 198; Dismissions and Doxologies, 218; Supplement (Infant School Hymns) 223–256.

Old Ohio Hymn Book. 1345. 458 *Hymns.*

"A Collection of Hymns and Prayers, for Public and Private Worship. Published by Order of the Evangelical Lutheran Joint Synod of Ohio, Zanesville. Printed at the Lutheran Standard Office, 1845." The Preface is signed by "The Hymn Book Committee," without date, and says: "The publication of this book was called for by the unanimous voice of the Evangelical Lutheran Synod of Ohio. The increasing demand for hymn books; the difficulty of obtaining them from the East; the very high price at which they were usually sold; and above all the strange bias of many hymns in the book, hitherto used, induced the publication of the present work. A joint committee was appointed by the three branches of the above Synod," etc. They "endeavored so far as practical, to follow their instructions, viz: to make the General Synod's book * * the basis of the new selection. * * This book, in its arrangement, essentially differs, in some important features, from the Old Collection. The hymns were mainly selected from the hymn book published by the 'General Synod,' some were added from the hymn book of the Ev. Lutheran Synod of New York, a small number from the 'Common Prayer,' and a few from other sources. Had the Committee been less restricted in their choice, a better selection would have been made." * * "The Committee by no means claim infallibility for themselves, nor perfection for their work. As it is, they believe this book to be better adapted to the views and wants, and more acceptable to the members, of the congregations of the Ev. Lutheran Church in the West, than the Old Collection has been."

The book is identical in shape and size with the New York Collection, labelled on the back 'Lutheran Hymns,' and rather dimly printed on not the best paper. There are 6 pages of Title, Preface, &c., 353 of Hymns, 15 of First Lines, and 79 at the end, of Prayers, taken from the New York Book. Here is the Table of Contents:

I. Of God. 1. The being and perfections of God, Hymn 1; 2. Of the Trinity (see Doxologies,) 19; 3. The Works of God, 22; 4. Providence of God, 26; 5. Praise to God, 41. II. Fall and Depravity of Man, 54. III. Christ. 1. His Divinity, 65; 2. His Mission and Works, viz: Advent and Birth of Christ, 69; His Life and Example, 79; His Sufferings and Death, 85; His Resurrection and Ascension, 93; 3. Salvation through Him, 102. IV. Holy Spirit. 1. His Influence, 131; 2. Gospel Call, 138; 3. Repentance, 176; 4. Faith, 200. (This is a queer arrangement.) V. Means of Grace. 1. The Word of God, 206; 2. Baptism, 215; 3. The Lord's Supper, 221. VI. The Christian 1. His Conversion, 233; 2. His Duty and Graces, Prayer, Love to Christ, Confidence and Trust in God, Christian Graces, 246; 3. His various Relations, 287. VII. The Church. 1. General and Missionary Hymns, 313: 2. Public Worship, 320; 3. Pastoral, 336; 4. Confirmation, 343; 5. Congregational, 355. VIII. Consummation of things; 1. Death, 363; 2. Resurrection, 388; 3. Judgment and Eternity, 392. IX. Special Occasions; 1. The Seasons, 405; 2. The New Year, 411; 3. Morning and Evening, 417; 4. Sickness and Recovery, 429; 5. Public and National Blessings and Afflictions, 436; Collections, 446. X. Dismissions, 450; Doxologies, 454–458.

This arrangement is more churchly than anything we have had hitherto, (if we except the Tennessee book, which is rather a caricature of churchliness than the thing itself,) but not so much so as we might expect from the Ohio Synod, nor sufficiently so to satisfy that body in later years. Except the rather absurd placing of such subjective topics as Repentance and Faith under the purely objective head of "Holy Spirit," it is respectable enough: though it is better to honestly *express* the great Festival and Seasons, than merely to imply them. We do not see why people who believe in the facts which those names represent, should be afraid to come out and say Advent, Christmas, Epiphany, Passion, Easter, Pentecost. But our Ohio brethren have done that since.

The *matter* of this compilation deserves and demands no special notice, since it is taken almost entirely from the Collections of the General Synod and New York Synod. From those two volumes together four hundred and fifty very decent hymns might have been culled; but it was not so done here. The book is more distinctively orthodox than the New York one, and perhaps a very little warmer in feeling; and it is more rational and less unchurchly than the General Synod's 2d edition; but it is scarcely superior in literary merit to either. Many of the dull and heavy productions that abound in both are carried over, and add their weight to the Ohio volume. The compilers seem to have felt most sympathy for the New York book; and it, rather than the General Synod's, gives the prevailing tone; not in doctrine indeed, but in temper, style, and spirit. The few hymns from other sources are, in general an improvement. Of the four hundred and fifty-eight in this book, Watts gives 130, Doddridge 44, Steele 28, C. Wesley 13 only, Newton 11, Cowper 9, and Montgomery 6; the rest we have not counted.

West India Hymn Book, 1850, 150 *H.*

Though this scarcely comes within our present scope, it may be briefly noticed as a historical and literary curiosity. It is a small 24mo of 187 pages. "Hymns for the use of the Lutheran congregations in the Danish West India Islands. 'Let the word of Christ dwell in you richly,' &c. Col. III. 16. Copenhagen: Published by C. A. Reitzel, Printed by Bianco Luno, 1850." Overleaf is "Authorized by the Danish Government. At the end stands this note: "This Co lection was made by the Rev. J. K. Bagger, formerly of St. Croix. In part these Hymns are of original English composition, some are translated from the Danish, some also are borrowed from other collections." Contents: "Hymns of Praise and Thanksgiving, 1–56. I. God and his attributes, 1; II. Creation, 7; III. Providence, 9; IV. Redemption, 15; V. Christmas Hymns, 26; VI. The Sufferings and Death of our Lord, 31; VII. Easter Hymns, 36; VIII. The Ascension of our Lord, 40; IX. Christ the Lord governing his Church, 43; X. The Holy Ghost and the Gospel Word, 47; XI. Eternity, 53. Hymns of Prayer and Supplication, 57–150. I. True Christianity, 57; II. Repentance, Faith and Forgiveness of Sins, 64; III. Love to God and

Confidence in Him, 74; IV. Brotherly Love, 87; V. Following Christ, 91; VI. Diligent use of the Word of God, Watching and Praying, 97; VII. Holy Baptism, 112; VIII. Holy Communion, 115; IX. Death, Resurrection, Judgment, 121; X. Hymns for Particular Occasions, 127–150; viz: For the King, 127, Confirmation, 128, Prayers of Intercession, 133, Catechising, 136, For the Sick, 138, Consecration of a Church, 140, End of the Year, 141, New Year, 142, Marriage, 145, For the Sunday Schools, 147, Conclusion 149, The Litany (prose) 150.

But 33 hymns of the 150, so far as we can see, are of English origin, being from Watts, Tate and Brady, and various sources. Some of the translations are from German originals, possibly through a Danish medium; and a few seem to be taken from Psalmodia Germanica and the Moravian books. The bulk of matter, we suppose, was "done into English" by the editor or his friends; and reads like the work of an educated man, not perfectly familiar with the language (though rather more so than Dr. Kunze and his assistants), and with a tolerable knack at rhyme and metre. The *matter*, as is almost always the case with our native Lutheran hymns, is excellent; solid, pure, and warm, far beyond the run of our English lyrics; the offspring and exponent of a rational, wholesome, and live Christianity. Here is a nice little Christmas verse, concise and to the point:

The angels bring good news to-day: We can our kindest Father name,
  "To you is born a Saviour,"   His Son our loving Brother.
Who will us from the crooked way   His heaven is now our native home,
  Of sin and death deliver.   His Church has unto us become
And God from whom the angels came   A dear and holy mother.

One of the Redemption or Advent hymns begins thus:

  Zion, rise! O earth, rejoice!   Branches scatter in his way,
Lo, to thee thy King is coming!   At his feet thy garments lay;
  To his praise prepare thy voice,   Thus with song and jubilation
In his footsteps joy is blooming.   Hail the King of thy salvation.

The first and last verse of an Easter Hymn:

O let the world of gloomy death   My days on earth may quickly pass;
  Its own sad message carry;   I fear not, death, thy power;
In Jesus will we place our faith,   The strength of man fades like the
  And gladly with him tarry.   grass,
He is our true and strongest Friend,   His beauty like a flower.

Who will us all 'gainst death defend,
Lead us to life and glory.

But if I trust, O God, in Thee,
Thou from my grave shalt quicken me
Dust only dust can cover.

From a Communion Hymn of considerable beauty :

Jesus, to taste thy delicious communion
Is now the longing of spirit and heart ;
Keep me from all that withholds from thy union,
Draw me to Thee ; my Beginning Thou art,
Show me how sin my heart sorely hath rended,
Show me the gulf of perdition in me,
That my bad nature to death may be bended,
And I in spirit may live but for Thee.

Hear Thou, O Jesus, thy dove which grieveth,
Shepherd, O seek for thy lamb led astray ;
Be to my thirst as a grape that relieveth,
Cleanse Thou my heart from defilement, I pray.

Teach me to worship the letter no longer,
Which makes but outwardly honest and fine ;
Give me to thirst after Thee and to hunger,
That I may call myself finally thine.

Let me, O Jesus, not call on Thee vainly !
Hungry, exhausted, and faint is my soul,
Saviour, Immanuel, show thy face plainly ;
Then shall my wounds and my sores be made whole.

Once Thou didst answer : "They might indeed languish,
If I would send them now fasting away ;"
Wouldst Thou suffer that now in my anguish,
Wanting thy food, I should faint in the way ?

This, "For the Sunday Schools," is admirable :

Dearest Lord, we come to Thee ;
We are ignorant, but Thou wilt teach us,
We are poor, but graciously
With thy heavenly gifts Thou wilt enrich us.

We are weak, but Thou, O Lord,
Mercifully wilt and canst defend us ;

And we know it from thy Word,
That the Holy Spirit Thou wilt send us.

Be our Shepherd good ! O may
We obey thy blessed voice for ever,
Dark and dangerous is our way :
Guide Thou us to life's eternal river

This, for "Catechising," has a very sweet simplicity :

Lord, Thou art the Truth and Way;   Oh, Thou all our frailty know'st.
Guide us, lest we go astray.   In ourselves we cannot trust,
Lord, Thou art the Life: by Thee   Send Thou us thy Holy Ghost.
May we gain eternity.

These are the right sort of thing in substance. The difficulty is to get a casket worthy of the jewel; and in transferring foreign hymns to our English tongue, to have form fitting with the spirit, the expression not sinking far below the ideas When this is obviated, and we can find renderings that are satisfactory and singable, these sweet songs from poets of our own communion across the water will make most precious additions to our hymnology, and help us not a little to recover the faith of our fathers.

General Synod's New Edition, 1850.

This differs from the book now in use only in "some mistakes that had been made as the work was passing through the press," which were corrected in the latter. We quote from the "Advertisement to the Large Edition" of 1852: "the most material of these is the substitution of new hymns in place of Nos. 357, 775, and 926, the first having been inserted by a mistake of the printer, and the others being duplicates of Nos. 60 and 415." These are marked ††.

General Synod's Revised Edition, 1852, 1024 *Hymns*.

We suppose Drs. Reynolds, Baugher, and Schmucker to have been the sub-committee who got this into its present shape. To them we owe it, that the official book of the Church is not positively absurd and indecent; that it would not now be easily mistaken for a compilation in the interest of the Hard-shell Baptists, or adapted to the use of negro camp-meetings. For difficult as it may be to praise the work on its own intrinsic merits, there is room for no little satisfaction and thankfulness, when we compare it with its predecessor. The best thing would have been for the Committee to have made a new book altogether; but since the constituted authorities could not, or would not do that, it was vastly better to have an imperfect reform than none at all. The changes, so far as they go, are for the most part great improvements: the most crying nuisances in the old editions are abated: the profane and pernicious matter which we thought it our duty to expose in earlier pages of this article, is, with much more only less glaring in deformity, thrown out, and its place supplied by matter always decent and often really good : and though these alterations constitute but one-fifth of the volume, a great advance in the style, temper, and churchliness of the work is thereby gained. In the body of the book (Hymns 1–766) there are forty-nine new pieces, displacing as many old ones. Ten are from the German ; Nos. 17, 43, 62, 70, 85, 220, 245, 341, 352, 357. The others are 90, 93, 98, 121, 134, 184, 197, 208, 213, 214, 226, 281, 306, 308, 330, 353, 411, 412, 415, 425, 463, 481, 512, 513, 537, 545, 558, 560, 576, 588, 594, 601, 657, 681, 694, 713, 724, 725, 726, 749. Several others are marked (†) as being new, which are not. Of the former Appendix, about one hundred hymns, or one-half, were retained; the rest being treated with the contempt they deserved. Thus about eight hundred and sixteen hymns in this Revised Edition are old, while the remaining two hundred and eight (including Doxologies) are added here. For the authorship (we give an approximate merely, not a statement of precise and full correctness,) Watts gives 182, C. Wesley 56, Steele 50, Doddridge 43, Newton 39, Montgomery 30, Cowper 24, the Stennetts 17, Beddome 12, Kelly 12, Fawcett 12, Heber 9, Needham 8, Collyer 8, Toplady 7, S. F. Smith 7, Hart, Barbauld, Kirke White, and Hoskins 6 each, and a vast variety of versifiers, known and unknown, of small merit and none at all, the remainder. About thirty-five are from the German, and two (one of them not generally known as such) from the Latin.

The *title* which all the editions of this have borne, "Hymns Selected *and Original*," or, as we find it in some copies,"*Original and Selected*," would, if it meant anything, imply that a fair proportion of the contents,—one-half, one-third, one-fifth,—were "original." It does *not* mean anything, being simply an absurd misnomer. We suppose there is nothing in the book which claims to be "original," except those hymns from Dr. Schmucker's pen, (two of which appeared in the original edition of 1828, the other in the Appendix of 1841,) and five German translations by Dr. Reynolds. Though Dr. Schmucker's mind is not commonly supposed to be of the poetical order, his verses, here presented, are very respectable in matter and form. The first of them, No. 456, we always liked. It will not do to sing it in Church, and some of the rhymes are negligent; but there is enough force of thought, tenderness of sentiment, and simplicity of expression, to make it a very pretty little poem.

It is, we think, of German origin. In Lyra Germanica, vol. 1. p. 161, is a piece whose original perhaps suggested it. The others, 555 and 898, for ministerial meetings and the like, are very fair; from the New School point of view, excellent. "Original" hymns are usually trash; but these are better than one-third, and as good as three-fifths, of the Collection. Dr. Reynold's translations (776, 794, 843, 965, 966,) are well enough in their way; but only one of them (776), we think, is worthy of the Church's use. That one is not wonderful, though, for want of a better, it will do, being simple in style and singable in metre.

The insertion of thirty hymns from the German was a confessed experiment, and has proved a notorious failure. With very few exceptions as to piece, place, or time, they are never sung, and never can be. And on the basis of this fact, many people, no doubt, have thought and said, "See the impossibility of employing translated hymns in our English worship, and the uselessness of attempting it!" Not a bit of it; nothing of the kind is proved or made probable. The impossibility of singing Dr. Mills' versions may be shown, and the uselessness of attempting to introduce such metres as those of hymns 17, 352, 794, 819, 858, which are not like anything that we Americans know or wish to know; but no more. The translations are not good enough; not at all worthy, in force and grace, in fire, dignity, and tenderness, of their originals; and most of them appear in a metrical form adapted to repel interest and admiration. Moreover, the German originals are not generally the ones best in themselves, or best adapted to our purpose. Perhaps the compilers did as well as they could at that time: but the experiment has not been fairly tried. Miss Wentworth's precious volumes had not then appeared, nor their admirable complement by an unknown hand, "Hymns from the Land of Luther:" and Miss Cox's valuable little work was scarcely known on this side the Atlantic. So the editors were reduced to the "Horæ Germanicæ" (Auburn, 1845) of Dr. Mills, who, however excellent a man and professor, was no poet: and to such additions as they might themselves make to order. Now that a thing was not done successfully at one time and by one man or set of men, does not prove that it cannot or will not be accomplished, under more favorable auspices, by others. Translations from the German need no more be stiff, dull, heavy, or unsingable, than original lyrics. Many translations are all this, and so are many native En-

glish verses. But that it is possible for a translation to pos
sess all the ease, grace and vigor that we can desire, may
appear from several hymns even in the General Synod's
book, where but one of them is credited as a translation.
What nobler songs of praise and prayer have we than 788,
from "O Haupt voll blut und wunden;" 180, "O Du
allersüste Freude;" 72, a part of "Befiehl du deine wege?"
No. 357 in the old edition, displaced by Mills' feeble imitation of that grand hymn, "Ich habe nun den Grund gefun-
den," was John Wesley's version of the same, a piece as
noble and inspiring as the other is grovelling and lifeless.
If the General Synod's Sub-Committee had been content to
do without precise correspondence of metre, they might have
taken from John Wesley some twenty German hymns, graceful, vigorous, and majestic. But they sacrificed the spirit to
the letter, and thereby achieved a failure the more disastrous,
as it would inevitably be taken to teach some lessons which
are not true, foster prejudices against what must be the line
of march, progress and reform, and all our future hymnology,
and so increase the difficulty of really doing, at a late day,
what had been here undertaken.

We have as little inclination as may be to undertake the
cheerless and almost useless task of pointing out the many
faults of the present Collection as a whole. The labor would
be herculean, and thankless. The powers that be will not
see those faults, or, if they see, will not attempt to remedy
them. When anything is hinted against the book, its parti-
sans are apt to reply, with an air of letting no more to be
said about the matter, that there are a great many good
hymns in it. Of course there are; it could not well be otherwise. Say there are 30,000 hymns in the English language; if one were to write the first line of each of these
on a separate slip of paper, put them all into a hat, draw out
1000 at random, and therewith make a hymn book; it would
doubtless contain some very good hymns. There will inevitably be some very good hymns in a collection, unless one
takes express pains to keep them out. But *there ought to
be nothing else.* A complete hymn book ought to contain
all the really good hymns in the language; and no hymn
book should contain *any but* good hymns. Simple and self-
evident as this rule may appear, we do not know an instance
in which it has begun to be carried out, scarcely one in which
it seems to have been recognized in theory. Certainly such
a rule had nothing to do with the getting up of the General

Synod's Collection. No one who has half an eye for poetry, or pretends to know cobble-stones from diamonds, will undertake to deny that that compilation contains a good deal of trash and twaddle, and a great deal of dreary drowsy doggerel. This, for example, is impressive: (No. 223.)

"Our days, alas! our mortal days,   'Evil and few,' the patriarch says,
  Are short and wretched too;   *And well the patriarch knew.*"

Another sample, No. 409:

"The wandering star and fleeting The morning cloud and early dew
    wind,   Bring our inconstancy to view."
Both represent the unstable mind:

Likely enough they do, and it is very proper they should: but what have these facts to do with our songs of praise to almighty God? Does He need to be instructed in the rudiments of every-day knowledge? Or do we presume, under pretence of addressing Him in humble worship, to fling these dull didactics at the head of our fellow-sinners? There should be a fitness in all things, but there is none in drawling out these loose, lazy, lifeless moralities to the Omniscient. Here is another stanza from the same effusion (409.)

"We sin forsake, to sin return;   In deep distress, then raptures feel,
Are hot, are cold, now freeze, now We soar to heaven, then sink to
    burn: hell."

Is that praise? Is it prayer? Is it worth dwelling on, here and thus? If the matter of it be expressed at all, it should be done in another spirit, and a vastly different style. "God," said Toplady, in the Preface to his Psalms and Hymns, "is a God of truth, of holiness, *and of elegance;* and He should be worshipped accordingly." Too generally is this forgotten; too seldom have orthodox believers attempted to attain in things pertaining to the service of God's house, the wisdom of the serpent. A gentleman, says the Autocrat of the Breakfast Table, will never be more a gentleman than in his hymns and prayers. We object, and we think with abundant reason, to whatever forces men upon a lower plane and level, in their communion with their Maker, than they are fit for and entitled to: to whatever necessities the use of rough, uncouth, incongruous, heavy, unmeaning, lame, or languid matter—whether prose or verse, extempore or liturgic—in our prayers and praises. In the olden days, nothing which had a blemish could be offered to the Lord.

We of the New Dispensation sometimes take too much advantage of our freedom from the letter of the law. If whatever is worth doing be worth doing well, our hymnology is in a sad and disgraceful state: for we insult the Most High with much that is unfit for human use!

The principles involved in these remarks apply to nearly all the standard Church Hymn Books in existence. The General Synod's does not stand alone, nor is it the worst: the Dutch and German Reformed Collections, we think, reach even a lower abyss of misery. But that is their fault, not our virtue; and their wretchedness does not make us better. It is a stubborn and obnoxious fact, that the Hymn Book now used by probably four-fifths of the English Lutheran Churches in America would be improved by throwing out one-half its contents, even were nothing added in their place. There is no use to multiply examples, or adduce further arguments; any one, who is not blind, must see the state of things. Fortunately many of our ministers are not particular, while their people are patient, and will sing—or let the choir sing—anything that is given out with enviable placidity.

The *arrangement* of the volume is worse, if possible, than the selection. That it is utterly unchurchly, must be seen at a glance: that it is illogical, appears from the Scriptures preceding their Author, and Christian Experience coming before the Church and the Means of Grace: that it is extremely inconvenient, every one who has used the book knows to his cost. Who, without the greatest waste of time and trouble, can find anything that he wants under such a heading as "Christian Experience," where one and twenty-eight lyrics are thrown together with scarcely a pretence of grouping or natural succession? Who can easily hit upon such a phase or treatment of the subject as he requires, when "The Kingdom and Church of Christ" contains seventy effusions, two-thirds of them utterly worthless, strewn together in admired confusion? The book produces, on an impartial mind which seeks to study and use it, the effect of a tangled wilderness, where some few fruits and flowers grow indeed, but so interwoven with and choked by thorns and thistles, that they barely repay the trouble of discovering them.

We think it our duty, before leaving the subject, to give an instance or two of the utter carelessness with which the book was put together; the lack of anything like conscientious thoroughness and attention to the work. Though the

Committee state, in the preface, that they "threw out all duplicates," no less than *four* such remain. See hymns 588 and 910, 578 and 903, 37 and 771, 724 and 986. This offence is not unfrequent among hymn books; but we do not know another which commits it to such an extent. Again; hymn 658, v. 4, prays that our children may, when adults, be baptized by immersion. A question naturally arises : if the compilers and revisers of a hymn book do not know what it already contains and do not look sufficiently into their admitted hymns to see whether the same contain doctrines directly contrary to their own belief and teaching,—how far are they fitted for their office, and how much good can be expected to come of their labors?

We might say something further, more weighty and important than anything we have yet urged. We might express briefly one chief result of a long, minute, and earnest study of the whole subject of English hymnology, in all its varying phases. We might say, not in the spirit of a special pleader, not in view of where we personally stand, or what we personally expect to do, but speaking, in all honesty, from serious conviction, the words of truth and soberness,— that the General Synod's hymn book, like most others, does not correctly and adequately represent the religion of the Lord Jesus. The idea of the Master is not worthily worked out, by these labors of his servants. One side, several sides, of Christianity may be here ; not the entire and beauteous whole. Some truths doctrinal and practical, some aspects of Christ's work and character, some phases of the spiritual life, may be here exhibited : others, to our view as important, as necessary, as fundamental, are passed by in silence. The Gospel has as it were been cut in two, and half of it is preserved in these English hymnals. Doubtless there is enough in this half to save us : so the Epistles without the Gospels might be enough to save us, or John and Matthew without Paul and Luke. But it is better to have the whole. The New School system, of which the General Synod is confessedly the embodiment and type, and its publications of course the exponents, is supposed to pride itself on its piety. Experimental religion, vital godliness, inward spirituality,—it has these or nothing. Now one thing that we consider specially unsatisfactory about the book before us, is just this point : its *piety.* In quality and degree, in size, shape, and complexion, in depth, earnestness, tenderness, solidity, simplicity, fervor,—it is deficient. There are many books of poetry that are much better devotional reading. The resources of pure hymnology afford material for an English volume that should tower above the General Synod's, in this respect alone, as Himalaya to an ash-heap, as Gulliver to the Lilliputians. The piety of the General Synod's Collection is neither so healthy, profound, ardent, lofty, nor consistent as the piety of a Christian hymn book ought to be and can be.

We might (we repeat it) unfold and enlarge upon the idea barely outlined in the last sentences: an idea startling perhaps to many, incredible no doubt to some. We might expand, enforce, illustrate, explain, apply : but we will not. One-half our readers would neither understand nor believe : and the rest, who need no such instruction, are in the way to have the want they feel supplied, and the reform they long for accomplished.

(*To be concluded.*)

ARTICLE V.

THE HAND OF GOD IN THE WAR.

By F. W. CONRAD, D. D., Chambersburg, Pa.

THERE is a God. As Creator he made all things by the word of his power; as Sovereign, he governs them by the Hand of his Providence. Accordingly, he worketh all things after the counsel of his own will, both in the armies of heaven and among the inhabitants of the earth. War is one of the most important and far-reaching events, which can occur in the history of nations. And as God exercises, both a general and a special Providence, in the affairs of individuals and nations, war cannot arise, continue, and end, without his knowledge, permission and control. And this is the truth, to a candid consideration of which we invite the attention of the reader under the theme: *The Hand of God in the War.*

I *The Hand of God is seen in the Origin of this War.* God created man, permitted his fall, and determined the development of his depravity. God redeemed man, made provision for his moral recovery, and enacted the law of benevolence, as the rule of his life. Now as human depravity and human redemption, stand in contrast with each other, so too, do they present developments, in direct opposition to each other. The development of man, under the promptings of depravity, is one of supreme selfishness; his development, under the influence of redemption, is one of disinterested benevolence. One of the grossest forms, in which human depravity exhibits its selfishness, is characterized by the Scriptures as man-stealing, which consists in subjugating man to a state of bondage, by the exercise of might in violation of right. To do this, is to treat man, in a manner directly contrary to the law of God, which enjoins upon each, to love his brother as himself. Man depraved, under the law of selfishness, craves freedom for himself, and imposes Slavery upon his fellow-man redeemed, under the law of benevolence, claims Liberty for himself, and demands Liberty for his fellow.

The Signers of the Declaration of Independence, under the light of Revelation, and the guidance of the law of benevolence, announced: "These truths to be self-evident; that all men are created equal; that they are endowed by their Creator, with certain inalienable rights, among which are, life, liberty, and the pursuit of happiness." This constitutes the American declaration of personal independence. It is the authoritative announcement of the political equality of all men. It is the self-evident expression of the true idea of the inalienable rights of human nature. It is the *Magna Charta* of Liberty.

Alexander H. Stevens, the Vice-President of the so-called Confederate States, has announced the declaration of slavery, practically adopted by them. It is made in these words; "The prevailing ideas, entertained by Jefferson, and the most of the leading Statesmen, at the time of the formation of the Constitution, were, that the enslavement of the African, was in violation of the law of Nature; that it was wrong in principle, socially, politically, morally. Those ideas, however, were fundamentally wrong. They vested upon the assumption of the equality of the races. This was an error. Our new government is founded on exactly the opposite ideas. Its foundations are laid, its corner-stone rests upon the great truth, that the negro is not equal to the white man; that slavery—subordination to the white race—is his natural and

THE

EVANGELICAL
QUARTERLY REVIEW.

NO. LXIII.

JULY, 1865.

and announced to the Church as legitimately elected and
called ; for by this rite Moses, Deut. 34, designated and announced to the people the call of Joshua as his successor :
that by this rite the person called might be confirmed in his
confidence that the call is legitimate and divine, and at the
same time be admonished that he is destined, dedicated and
as it were devoted to the ministry and service of God ; so
hands were laid upon the victims, and so Joshua was confirmed in his vocation : that it might be a kind of public and
solemn protestation of the Church before God, that the form
and rule prescribed by the Holy Spirit in regard to the elec-
tion and vocation were complied with ; so Paul tells Timothy, 1 Tim. 5, to lay hands suddenly on no man, neither be
partaker of other men's sins ; that by this visible rite it
might be declared that God approves the call which was made
by the voice of the Church ; for as by the voice of the Church
God elects ministers, so by the testification of the Church he
approves the vocation ; so the vocation of deacons was approved, Acts 6, and hence it is that God dispenses grace
through the imposition of hands : and in prayer, when it is
designed especially to invoke the name of the Lord upon
any person, hands are usually laid upon him, for he is,
as it were, offered to God and set before him, prayers being
offered that God would be pleased to bestow his grace and
blessing on him ; so Jacob laid his hands upon the children
whom he blessed, Gen. 48, so the elders laid their hands upon
the sick and prayed, James 5, and so Christ laid his hands
upon the babes and blessed them, Mark 10.   *   *   And

this earnest prayer, in the ordination of ministers, is not in vain, because it is founded upon the divine command and promise. This is what Paul says : 'The gift which is in thee by the putting on of my hands.' " Exam. II, 221. Thus it is seen that the call is not given, but simply confirmed, by ordination, which is an ecclesiastical rite that is not indispensable, but that is, nevertheless, of great utility.

This article completes our essay on the Christian Ministry. The doctrine exhibited is dear to those who would be faithful to the word of our blessed Lord, and continue in the way of our honored fathers. They cannot otherwise than contend earnestly for the faith, once delivered to the saints, and protest solemnly against those hierarchical tendencies which, being so congenial to man's natural inclinations, seem to be spreading, even within our own Church, with fearful rapidity. It is for common Christian rights and privileges, secured to believers by our common Christian faith, that we are pleading, and we cannot be indifferent to the success of our plea. We are confident of its truth, and to the God of truth we commend it. May he bless it, without whose blessing all is vanity ; and may he make it instrumental in leading souls to prize their precious privileges and inalienable rights, as kings and priests unto God, through faith, to whom he has been pleased to give the keys of the kingdom of heaven ; that the Church may be faithful to her Lord, and the ministers not ashamed, while they are servants of the Lamb, to be servants, also, of the Lamb's Bride ! "We preach not ourselves, but Christ Jesus the Lord ; and ourselves, your servants for Jesus sake." 2 Cor. 4 : 5.

ARTICLE II.

LUTHERAN HYMNOLOGY.

By Rev. F. M. Bird, A. M., Philadelphia.

The Evangelical Psalmist. 1859. 962 *Hymns.*

As the music, which is the chief feature of this publication, does not come within our scope, and as the hymns are substantially the same with those of the General Synod's

Collection, it calls for very little in the way of critical notice: and it is too well known to need any formal description, or account of its surface facts. All who read this article are likely to know that Drs. Seiss, McCron, and Passavant were the authors, and made changes enough from the G. S., the basis of their labors, to constitute a distinctly new book, though closely related to the old one.

The principal changes were as follow: 143 hymns in G. S. were omitted, 91 of them being in the body of the book and 52 in the Appendix: while 98 new pieces were added. (This enumeration does not include the Doxologies, which in the Psalmist are scattered over the last seven pages, and are not numbered.) Many of the additions were gain, many others were scarcely worth having. The majority of the omitted hymns were better out than in; though some few of them were a serious loss, as 180, "Holy Ghost, dispel our sadness," which the compilers may not have known to be from the German. Of the translations which form so prominent a feature in the G. S., eleven only are retained. Being what they are, all might have been dropped but two, and no harm done. Taken all in all, these changes in the text constitute, as might be expected, a manifest improvement: though they neither leave the old book, nor make a new one. It is that anomalous and unsatisfactory thing, a hybrid.

But the *arrangement* of the Psalmist is something which we can contemplate with decided satisfaction. No compromise or half-way work was attempted here, but a thorough and radical reform. The immense subject of "Christ," undivided and unarranged in G. S., is here parceled into six appropriate and natural subdivisions, and "Christian Experience" into eight: "Adoration and Praise" begin the volume, and "The Word" is put where it belongs, as a Means of Grace. Although the editors were encumbered with tunes upon the page, they produced an order of sequence so far superior to that of their predecessors, that even if they had kept the *matter* of the book unchanged, the Psalmist would, for all practical purposes, be worth the General Synod's Collection twice over.

The new "Table of Contents" implies a mild effort to improve the churchliness of the work. So mild, that it does not extend beyond said table; for the omissions and additions do not specially affect the character of the book, one way or another. Taking into account the position and views of its compilers (or of two of them at least), the book is a fair sample of how little correct tendencies and virtuous inclinations can accomplish towards a reformation of our hymnology, in the absence of precedents and helps, of acknowledged codes and models. Where the Psalmist, with its accompanying "Church Forms," is used, we have the anomaly of churches very tolerably Lutheran in the order and style of worship for the rest, but singing constantly—unless the minister have wit and grace to keep a large proportion of the hymns in the background—matter which, if not anti-Lutheran, will be often un-Lutheran, mildly puritanic, methodistic, or humanitarian. The compilers of the Psalmist made no small improvements on what had been before; but greater improvements must be made yet, before we can reach our true ideal Hymnology.

New Ohio Collection. 354+7 *Hymns.*

The original preface to this book is not dated (a very wrong practice by the way) and we know not in what years the first and second editions appeared. The third has a note dated 1858, and the fourth came out in 1863.

The copy before us is smaller than the edition of 1845, and about the size of the General Synod's 24mo.: back labeled as before, "Lutheran Hymns." Pages VIII, 330. No "Prayers" in this edition. Title, excepting that item, as before: "Collection of Hymns for Public and Private Worship. Published by order of the Evangelical Lutheran Joint Synod of Ohio. Fourth Edition. Columbus: J. W. Osgood, Printer. 1863."

In some respects this is the best book we have yet had; it is certainly the most churchly. But of that presently. The preface states that it is new, prepared "without special reference to any particular hymn-book now in use, and with a view to meet, as nearly as practicable, the views of the churches in their connection." This is the only right way. While we are tied down to the past, and hampered by all the blunders and failures of our predecessors, we can do but a half or quarter work. This patching up old books, so that the two can be used together, according to the prefaces, but not according to the facts, is a poor business. If a book is good, be satisfied with it: if merely insufficient, add a supplement; if inherently bad, throw it away and make a better.

The arrangement is bold and striking: none of our books have grouped their contents under so few large heads. Thus:

I. Praise to God, No. 1. II. Works and Providence of God, 11. III. Redemption : 1. Fall and Depravity of Man, 23 ; 2. The Redeemer, 33 ; 3. Grace, 47 : 4. Gospel Call, 54 ; 5. Penitence, 64 ; 6. Faith, 72 : 7. Justification, 80. IV. The Church : 1. In General, 97 ; 2. Public Worship and Lord's Day, 107 ; 3. Pastoral, 121 ; 4. Congregational, 125 ; 5. Confirmation, 131 ; 6. Missionary, 135. V. Festivals : 1. Advent, 138 ; 2. Nativity, (Christmas) 145 ; 3. New Year, 152 ; 4. Epiphany, 154 ; 5. Passion, (Good Friday) 155 ; 6. Easter, 164 ; 7. Ascension, 170 ; 8. Pentecost, (Whitsunday) 174 ; 9. Trinity, 182 ; 10. Reformation, 190. VI. The means of Grace : 1. The Word of God, 194 ; 2. Baptism, 204 ; 3. The Lord's Supper, 212. VII. The Christian : 1. Holiness and Prayer, 227 ; 2. Various Relations and Affections, 242. VIII. Special Occasions : 1. The Family and Schools, 267 ; 2. National Relations, 289 ; 3. Thanksgiving and the Seasons, 293 ; 4. Daily Devotion, 299. IX. Consummation : 1. Death, 325 ; 2. Resurrection, 339 ; 3. Judgment, 342 ; 4. Eternity, 344.

We do not quite like this. It is too arbitrary, even violent. Subjects are torn apart and put together somewhat too roughly, whether they will bear it or not ; the order of nature and reason is not enough followed. Penitence, Faith, and Justification are subjective matters, belonging to man ; we would not put them with the Fall, the Redeemer, and Grace, which properly group together about the objective head of Redemption. They belong rather in the neighborhood of, and just before, "The Christian." Of this last by no means enough is made. No one will accuse us of inclining too seriously towards the General Synod's mountain of "Christian Experience:" but the vast and varied subject of the Inner Life, Graces and Duties, Trials and Comforts, Trust and Love, require vastly more than forty hymns and two subdivisions. Be as churchly as we may, we must not forget that we are human. That humanity, frail and foolish as it is, our religion does and must recognize. The feelings and experiences that belong to our nature and condition, *must* come into a hymn-book. Let them be *admitted*, but not *emphasized*. Let us understand that they are not, and cannot be, our religion, or any part of it : and within that limit let them, as essential parts of our inevitable humanity, take hold on our religion as strenuously as they will. We do insist on this, and protest against any mistaken reform which would throw our humanity in the shade, and drive the many noble hymns of living faith, hope, love, sorrow, submission, consecration, aspiration, out of our books. If we mistake not, this is not the spirit of the unequalled German hymnology, nor of the Lutheran Church. And on this point we have a little quarrel with the Ohio book.

Again: to set down the Church Year simply as so many "Festivals," seems to us unworthy of the solemnity, importance, and value of the sacred seasons separately taken, and much more of the connected whole, of that grand chain of imperishable truth, that sweet succession of saving facts, that the noble condensation and completion of the gospel plan. Nor can we be contented to see a human Festal, however worthy, set beside those which are entirely of God. Precious as Reformation Day is to us, it should never be put in the same list with Christmas and Easter and Whitsunday.

We come now to the Contents. 51 hymns are from the German, many being new translations by members, we suppose, of the compiling committee. Nos. 23, 34, 46, 105, 106, 182, 188, 208, 209 are by Rev. M. Loy: 103, 189, 212, 218, 262, 266, 303 by Prof. L. Heyl: 225, by J. Salyards: 4 by J. H. Good (who these two were we know not). Dr. Mills is found worthy to constitute thirteen: five are taken from Dr. Reynolds, two of them original here, Nos. 1, 214: Dr. Alexander gives two, one not usually known, 143: one, 228, is from Anderson's, the Edinburgh translator (and a very poor one) of Luther's hymns: while five, marked as new here, 187, 231, 232, 241, and several more, are anonymous, being credited to various newspapers, etc. Besides these, there are a number of originals, not translations. M. Loy gives seven, Nos. 26, 207, 222, 223, 224, 239, 240, and Mr. Heyl one, 226. There are, moreover a number marked †, as not having been published in other English hymn-books. The "Churchman" gives six, "Church of England Magazine" three, "American Messenger" two, &c. Of these none are noticeable except Mr. Loy's, which are, of course, very churchly. The best, we think, is one on baptismal regeneration, (we see no reason to be ashamed of the name) No. 207.

At Jesus feet our infant sweet	We here embrace his proffered grace
We lay with all its stain,	In this baptismal wave,
That renders it for heaven unmeet	Nor shall the world our trust efface—
Until 'tis born again :	The bath its soul will save.

We fail to see the Holy Three
  Concealed the font within,
Mere water seems the mystery
  That cleanses us from sin :

But who can tell what virtues dwell
  Through God's word in that flood,
Or who the simple faith repel
  That owns it Jesus' blood ?"

There are some pretty steep expressions in that. The last line of the first verse, especially, we do not believe in at all. *Christ*, not his ordinance, saves the child's soul. But the piece has much force and some poetry, and we give it as a sample. No. 225, translated by "J. Salyards," from Woltusdorf, affords another instance of how a true, important, and comfortable doctrine may be misrepresented by perverse and exaggerated expressions. It is a Lord's Supper hymn. Thus begins verse 2 :

"Bread most holy let me bless thee!
For he mingles as I press thee,

Flesh divine, all rent and riven,
Wounds my guilty race has given,"
    &c.

If that be not Romanism, it is Consubstantiation, which is no Lutheran doctrine. There is no use of letting our good be evil spoken of.

The translations are perhaps better than the General Synod's, but are scarcely, in our opinion, a success. They are mostly not taken from the finest or most famous German hymns; the metres of many are unfamiliar; and their English dress is hardly such as to make them attractive and useful. The best perhaps (after the two by Dr. Alexander) are 34 and 188, by Rev. M. Loy, from Hiller and Selnecker :

"God, in human flesh appearing,
  Took the children to his breast,
Lambs with his green pastures
    cheering,
  Fitting for his heavenly rest;
This is gentleness unbounded,
  This is lowliness of heart;
All are by his love surrounded,
  None are ever bid depart."

"Let me be thine forever,
  My gracious God and Lord ;
May I forsake thee never,
  Nor wander from thy word :
Preserve me from the mazes
  Of error and distrust,
And I shall sing thy praises
  Forever with the just."

A book composed of one part matter like this, translations and originals, made or taken to suit their own views and purposes, and five parts of common English matter, made long before, with very different purposes and views, must of necessity be somewhat incongruous. We presume the Committee found it a troublesome and uncongenial task, to select the three hundred inevitable English hymns. This appears from the preface, where they felt "constrained to acknowledge, that, with more time, and a better field to select from, than our *rather barren English Hymnology,* their work could have been much improved, and brought into closer conformity with the peculiar wants of the Lutheran Church." The rather bold expression which we have underscored, is in one sense true, and in another not. Our English hymnology is not so rich as the German, in quantity or quality, in matter, meaning, spirit, or style, in thought, poetry, or devotion. A mind educated in, or brought to, the solid, pure faith of our Church, will find a dreary deficiency about most of our English lyrics; a lack of force, purity, simplicity, depth, earnestness,—some of these qualities, or all of them at once: these hymns do not say what we want said, nor say it as we would have it; they are cut after another pattern from ours, built on a different foundation, framed in accordance with other, and, as we think, less correct tastes: all this is true, and it is proportionably hard to make a really Lutheran hymn-book out of English materials, supplied by men who were Dissenters, Methodists, Calvinists, Anabaptists, every sort of creed but ours. Not that any thing in our hearts or belief prevents our joining in worship with any Christian brother of whatever name; but that the effusions of these said brethren do not correspond with, and come up to, our idea of what is right and just, and true and proper. In atmosphere, style, tone, temper, if not in matter, doctrine, verbiage, they do not meet our views. Here is the difficulty; and so far, if the Ohio compilers—and we with them—are right, our English hymnology is comparatively barren. But *positively* barren it is not. There is enough matter in it,—if one only knows where to find, and how to use the same,—which will fit our purpose very tolerably well. To the Ohio compilers it may have indeed been barren, but it is not necessarily so to every one. Their opportunities of knowing the range and capacity of English hymnology, were, we suppose, limited: it would certainly be possible to get three hundred English hymns better in themselves, and better adapted to fit with German translations in a Lutheran book, than those which they employed for that purpose. We incline to fancy that these gentlemen rather took for granted that it was a hopeless case, and paid no very special or deep attention to the matter; at any rate, had no faith in the possibilities of their work. Without such faith and such careful labor, a first-rate hymn-book can never be made. The Ohio book has its merits; it deserves careful and favorable attention, and we have given it such: but better things can be done on the same line, and the Church will see them done.

General Synod's Sunday School Hymns, 1860. 346+50 II.

It cannot be a greater relief to our readers than it is to us, to come across something which we can heartily and almost unqualifiedly commend. The little book before us is, for its purpose and in its place, really *good*. There are a few pieces in it which we would rather see out, as 146, 147 and 149: but the great body of the contents is more nearly right in character, spirit, style, tone, tendency, than is the case with anything else which we have had to notice. A cheerful and healthy atmosphere seems to pervade the work: the real wants of children have been kept in view, rather than some half-pagan system of impracticable and inhuman dogmas. The book has a freshness, simplicity, tenderness, heartiness, which is not unworthy of the relation a civilized Christian Church should maintain to her redeemed and baptized infants. The way in which the Festivals are brought out, moreover, marks an era of most happy progress in the right direction. We are almost surprised that so great an advance could be made on what went before. Revs. Albert and Titus, we believe, were the compilers; and their work speaks well for their heads and hearts. We do not understand how, with such a book, officially and of the Church, in existence, any Lutheran clergyman can think himself justified in using, instead, a more private publication, as

Kurtz's Sunday School Hymns. 1860. 435 *Hymns.*

This is an enlargement of the one published in 1843, which we noticed as Dr. Passavant's. As far as hymn 251, the stereotype plates of the old book were retained and used: beyond that is an Appendix, prepared by Rev. M. Sheeleigh. This part—except twenty hymns at the end, for "Revivals of Religion," which have no business in a Sunday School Hymn-book—is not open to the objections which we urged, with some earnestness, against the earlier portion. The Appendix contains too many, to our taste, of the loose rollicking lyrics which are commonly considered the best thing for young people to sing, but from which our official Sunday School book is happily almost free: but otherwise we have no special

fault to find with it. The amiable editor himself supplied
seven original pieces, Nos. 264, 286, 339, 375, 378, 380,
398. One item is very noticeable: under the number 340
stands, in lonely dignity, part of Miss Winkworth's vigorous
rendering of Luther's Christmas Carol.

"Welcome to earth, Thou noble   Thou com'st to share our misery:
    Guest,   What can we render, Lord, to thee?"
Through whom this wicked world
    is blest!

We mean no disrespect to Mr. Sheeleigh's labors, nor to our
English hymns in general: but the sight of this blessed
German heart-song, coming where it does, refreshes us as
springs in the desert, as the shadow of a great rock in a
weary land.

Kurtz's Infant School Hymns. 1860. 132 *Hymns.*

Sometimes bound up with the last, and sometimes published separately. It was prepared by Mr. Sheeleigh, and No.
116 is his. Infant hymns are scarcely open to criticism;
and we should think the half hundred added to the General
Synod's Sunday School book, were quite enough, but every
one to his taste.

St. John's S. S. Hymns. 1864. 75 *Hymns.*

"Select Hymns, for the use of St. John's Ev. Luth. Sunday School." (Dr. Seiss', Philadelphia.) Compiled by a
committee of teachers, not published, but privately printed,
exclusively for the use indicated. It is used in connection
with the General Synod's Sunday School book, especially on
Anniversaries, etc.

The Hymnal of the Future.

We have fulfilled our promise, and given an account, which
we at least intended to be fair, accurate, and full, of the English Lutheran Hymn-book of the past and present. Our
article has extended to a length we did not anticipate, and
taken up an amount of space and time which only the acknowledged importance of the subject could justify. We
might have said more, we might have said less. Whatever
we have said has been said in the interest of truth: and we
are glad to see—whether by expressions of assent or dissent
is of little moment—that our words have been the means of

drawing increased attention to the subject, and calling forth the sentiments of others thereupon. Let a matter be fully discussed, and the truth will appear. But "he is a poor reformer, who merely points out the faults of existing things, without suggesting a remedy;" and it may reasonably be expected of us to indicate the principles on which, in our view, a true, pure, genuine, sufficient collection,—the Hymnal of the Future,—shall be formed, and the leading features by which the same should be distinguished.

I. First, then, an essential prerequisite to the production of such a book is a *competent knowledge* of Hymnology by the compilers. Any man of sense would be apt, at first sight, to consider this a self-evident proposition. One would not make a spelling-book without first knowing how to spell; one does not publish a treatise, however elementary, on Botany or Conchology, unless he himself possessed at least the rudiments of the science. The rule holds in all things else; why not here? In almost every walk in life, for nearly every labor in the world, study, experience, acquaintance with the subject, aptness for the work, are considered necessary. We have too long dispensed with them here. For the last hundred years it has been customary, throughout Protestant Christendom, for whoever had a mind, (or for whoever, not having a mind, was appointed thereto by the constituted authorities,) to make a hymn-book; though he might know and care nothing about the facts or the principles of Hymnology, about who had written, what he had written, how he had written, and what use should be made of his writings. It is time we got beyond this; not only for the greater credit and honesty of dispensing with errors, misstatements, negligences, and ignorance; not merely to avoid the scandal of Christian men making, using, and offering to God careless and unworthy pieces, of work, such as they would disown and be ashamed of in their secular life: but because an English Hymn-book cannot be in any respect so good as it may and ought to be, unless its authors have a tolerably minute and thorough knowledge of the whole range of English hymnology. We know the difficulties of the study. The subject has not yet been reduced to a science; its principles are not yet digested, its theories not written down: there have been but a few slight and partial essays towards this. Of the *externals*, the facts, the materials, it is not possible at this day, and in this country, to have a com-

plete and exhaustive knowledge. Still we can do something.
Perfection may be unattainable, but we can approximate it.
There are in existence probably somewhat over one thousand
original volumes of hymns and similar sacred poetry, by their
various authors. These are the sources, fountains, authorities. Two or three hundred of them are of more or less
practical importance, as containing the hymns which have
been, are, might, could, would, or should be brought into use.
From these books alone we can get, with perfect accuracy,
the author's text, the original draft and shape of a hymn.
And by these alone can one ascertain what an author has
written, how much, and how well. It sometimes happens
that some of the best hymns, even of a distinguished writer,
have remained unknown and unused, and can be found only
in his original work : and more frequently that his own text
is, at least in some respects, better than the mutilated readings which are found elsewhere. Here are two advantages,
of the most direct and practical nature, resulting from this
examination of the sources. Moreover, there comes thus a
certain familiar intimacy with the men and materials one is
dealing with, an insight into the history and heart of the
subject. The careful student of these originals is no longer
a mere dabbler at the science, peeping from without into its
mysteries ; he has taken his degree and entered within the
shrine. He ceases to be a reaper of other men's harvests, a
compiler from other compilations. The first requisite for a
thoroughly good hymn-book is, that, abandoning this ignoble
dependence upon others, and using some freedom of investigation, it should take its materials, not second-hand from
anywhere as it happens, but (as far as possible) fresh from
the pages where they are found pure, primitive, legitimate,
and authoritative.
   But this is not all that must be done in pursuance of our
first rule. We must know not only what hymns have been
written, but what have been sung. We cannot afford to ignore any land-marks : we must see what our neighbors have
been about all this time, who, with more or less wisdom, energy, and comfort, are traveling the same road with us.
There are in the English language we know not what number,—probably three thousand, perhaps many more,—of
hymn-books, selections, collections, call them what you will.
These are important, not merely as containing many valuable
hymns, which appeared for the first time thus, and as giving

an infinite variety of new, and often improved, readings; but as presenting the life of English and American Christendom, past and present, in all its varying phases. Every operation and condition of the human mind, more or less under the Divine Spirit's influence; every shade of doctrinal belief, emotional temper, and ecclesiastical position; almost every shade of theology, exegesis, and even Church history, is either exhibited or indicated here. (And though the odd thousands be not within reach, yet several hundred, giving some idea of the subject on a small scale, may be found in a few private libraries in this country.) If, after faithful study of this varying and conflicting mass, one does not get at the truth, his mind must be either dull, narrow, or prejudiced. The wanderings of our brethren should point us to the true path; their partial darkness should help us to a fuller light. If "each man's life is all men's lesson," each hymn-book, however bad, may add a grain of instruction to the stock of him who would construct a better. "The proper study of mankind is man:" and they, who shall compile our ideal Hymnals of the Future, must find their proper study in the Hymnal of the Past and Present.

II. The second prerequisite is found in a severely correct judgment and thoroughly refined taste. Hymns, before being admitted, should be subjected to a much stricter criticism than has been the fashion. We do not mean that we would reject all which contain the first person singular of the personal pronoun, or change it to the plural: nor that we would cast out "There is a fountain filled with blood." because of the sensuous image in the first verse, or "How beauteous are their feet," on the ground that the feet of the minister, in some particular place, may not be literally beautiful. We do not mean that the compiler should employ any narrow, arbitrary, or absurd style of criticism; that his taste should be finical and prudish, and overly delicate; much the contrary. But he should have a lofty standard, loftier than has been known yet: that standard should embrace not merely literary and poetic excellence, (though these include more than is commonly thought;) but sense, force, doctrine, tone, temper, the whole character of the piece: his admitted hymns should, as a rule, come up to the standard: and there should be no exceptions to that rule, except for some sufficient reason. Sterorhold and Rouse might do for two hundred years ago; many of the hymns yet in our books were well enough

perhaps when they were written; but the world moves.
There are enough really good hymns, if one only knows two
things; first, where to find them; second, how to recognize
them when found. When a compiler has learned these two
rules well, he will have no need of poor or negative hymns
to eke out his book. Most American hymnals seem to have
no standard at all, but contain good, bad, and indifferent in
pleasing confusion, all sorts to suit all tastes. A happy exception is found in the Sabbath Hymn-book, by two Andover
Professors. 1858. It has a standard; and the consequence
is that nothing absurd or disgraceful is found within its
covers; all the contents reach a certain mark. But the mark
is not far enough up; the standard can and should be much
higher.

We have said that this standard includes not merely literary style and finish, but the spirit, tone, and what we must,
with the painful prospect before us of being again uncom-
prehended and objected to, again venture to call *doctrine.*
The true hymnal should have a manly, robust, large faith;
clear, positive views, joined with the broadest charity. It
should be liberal, not loose; enlightened, not emasculated;
catholic, not crazy. Its limits should be far from narrow,
but they should rigidly be guarded. A thing cannot be let
in simply because it is pretty, nor simply because it is pious.
Some of the finest sacred poems we have must be excluded,
because they either express views to which we cannot assent,
or breathe a spirit which we do not approve. For instance,
there is Charles Wesley's hymn, "Lord, I believe a rest remains." It is one of the most vigorous and elegant lyrics
which that eminent saint, and great poet, ever wrote; but it
is throughout a description of, and a prayer for, positive
perfection. Some non-Methodist books (not any of our Lutheran ones) retain part of this piece, uselessly, and not very
honestly trying to pretend that it refers to the heavenly rest:
which is a patent deception. The true hymnal cannot do
this sort of thing. It may regret to lose so fine a poem; it
may see that the tender and earnest beauty of these verses,
objectionable as they are, might sometimes be vastly edifying; but it has no right to do evil that good may come. And
here we bring up against a widespread delusion, that has
place in many respectable minds. It is often urged that
popularity is the highest tribunal, from which there is no appeal; that if a hymn be acceptable, and people find or fancy

it useful, that gives it effectual sanction. By no means. Things in themselves abominable, may often have done good. We have no doubt that some of those peculiar productions, which we thought it necessary to criticise in our second article, have frequently been useful. We think it likely that sinners have been hopefully converted by the late Elder Knapp's favorite piece :

> "Good morning careless sinner: for you I am alarmed :
> Why are you not afflicted, or why not dead and damned ?"

Now if we are to keep everything that anybody sees fit to like and to fancy useful, especially at camp-meetings, what an unmeasured mess of nonsense, and far worse, we shall have ; and what a terrible amount of harm will be done along with the good ! No : people can learn to be moved and edified as well by good poetry as by doggerel, and to get and hold their religion in a sound, healthy, rational way, as easily as through fanaticism and excitement. Cannot people see that it is not a mere matter of expediency, but a plain question of right and wrong ? If a thing be in itself amiss, we have no right to do it, no matter what we, our neighbors, or the Church, may gain thereby. God has given us taste and judgment, as much as he has anything else; and they are to be a sort of intellectual conscience to us. And therefore we insist that they must be used in their "finest, keenest, largest, and most concentrated action," in the making of the ideal hymn-book.

III. The last prerequisite is a thoroughly broad, liberal, appreciative, catholic spirit. Those who would compile the true Hymnal must not be bigots or sectarians. No narrow exclusiveness, no undue attachment to some favorite forms of truth, should blind their eyes or close their hearts to the merits of whatever is excellent, in whatever way. They should be able to turn and apply the ancient motto: *"Christianus sum : nihil Christiani a me alienum puto :* to seek truth in the most unpromising quarters, to acknowledge it readily and gladly, wherever found. Our Presbyterian brethren, if they wish to improve their hymn-books, must stop throwing into the background the American Charles Wesley ; and High Anglicans should modify their contempt of Watts and Doddridge, though they were Dissenters. We ought all to learn, that Hymnology is a thing almost as broad as Christianity ; and that is much larger than any of us know. Accordingly we should be thankful rather than

frightened, if the Unitarian, Sir John Bowring, and the De-
ist, Helen Maria Williams, have given us one or two hymns
fit to use. On the same principle we must get rid of our
personal prejudices, and be willing to believe that the hymns
which we have been fond of, and accustomed to, may not be
the only good ones, nor the best, in existence. We must get
rid of a notion which many people, knowing precisely nothing about the matter, have deeply imbibed, and are disposed
strenuously to insist upon : that translated hymns, whether
German, Latin, or what, can be of no use ; that we must
keep nearly to what we have ; that our real resources are
confined to what has been, or shall be, produced of purely
English origin, and chiefly to such as have already received
the Church's sanction, and are more or less known and popular. This, as we shall see by and by, is an utter mistake.
A spirit thoroughly appreciative and catholic must, perforce,
be independent : it will recognize and bring into use many
hymns which spirits less catholic, and less appreciative, have
failed to use or to recognize. In the songs above, there is
no distinction of time or nation, but David and Isaiah join
with Clement and Ephraim, with Gregory and Ambrose, with
Luther and Gerhard, with Watts and Wesley. There should
be as much as possible of this in the songs below. In the
ideal Hymnal, there *must* be something of it. The religious
views and practices, the style of thought and feeling which
prevail in one course of the world and at one particular
hour,—these are not catholic Christianity, only a small part
of it. It is not what *we* think, but what others think too :
not merely what is held *now*, but what has been held since
the Day of Pentecost. Doubtless this is the greatest and
wisest of the ages, but every age thought that of itself, before us. The last eighteen centuries have been Christian
ones, and some respect is due to all of them. It is not only
the primitive days, nor the Lutheran Reformation, nor the
Wesleyan Revival, nor the present time of activity in missions, literature and speculation : we should give a hearing to
every period, and take something from each. The true system, no matter in what, is eclectic. There never yet was a
creed or a communion, a set of men, a phase of thought, or
an array of customs, that monopolized God's truth and
Christ's grace. Yet some have had far more of these, others
far less, than their neighbors. By carefully and honestly
studying these, dividing the tares from the wheat, rejecting
that which is evil and keeping what seems pure, we are likely

to come as near as human nature may, with its present opportunities, to the ideal Truth. And on these principles
ought the ideal hymn-book to be constructed.

These, then, are the prerequisites for a thoroughly good
Hymnal: competent knowledge of the subject, severely correct taste and judgment, and warm, appreciative catholicity
of spirit. The first will ensure that nothing is overlooked;
the second, that nothing is unworthily admitted; the third,
that nothing is rejected without a reason. No human work
can expect to attain positive perfection: but a Hymnal in
whose preparation these rules were implicitly obeyed, might
reasonably expect to be, not only much better than any that
we have yet, but as good as can well be made now. Some
of the characteristics of such a book appear plainly enough
for the mere enumeration of their first principles: it would
be more complete than any collection extant, yet not so large
as most: it would be entirely tasteful and pure: it would
contain all the really good hymns in the language, and no
others. But we need to give some further description of
what the true Hymnal should be, according to our notion.

The *Arrangement* should be more natural, logical, and
convenient than we are accustomed to. The subjects should
follow and run into one another of their own accord, so that
if one knows what he wants, he should know where to find it,
with no other help than the one general Table of Contents.
The two grand natural divisions, of the Objective and the
Subjective, or God's part and man's, should apportion the
book between them. Under the first of these the headings
should run somewhat as follows: the great facts which save
us being placed mainly where they belong, under the Church
Year, and there presented far more fully and worthily than
has yet been done in any American hymn-book.

I. General Hymns of Worship. A. Praise and Thanksgiving; B. General Petition; C. Lord's Day and Public
Worship. II. Divine Nature. III. Creation and Providence. IV. Sin and Redemption. V. Advent. VI. Christmas. VII. New Year. VIII. Epiphany. IX. Example
and Teaching of Christ. X. Passion. A. The Lenten
Season; B. Passion Week; C. Good Friday; D. Easter
Eve. XI. Easter. XII. Ascension. XIII. Christ's Glory,
Kingdom, and Priesthood. XIV. Jesus Hymns (hymns of
praise and praise to Christ, of communion with him; hymns
dwelling upon his person, name, office, etc.) XV. Pentecost,

XVI. Trinity. XVII. The Church. A. Her Foundation and Nature; B. Her Persecution and Protection; C. Communion of Saints; D. Ordination, Ministerial Occasions, Dedication, etc.; E. Missions. XVIII. A. The Word; B. Baptism and Confirmation; C. The Lord's Supper. The immense advantage of much of this arrangement will be felt by those who know how to value and observe the Church Year worthily, and who have felt painfully the lack of sympathy with their own views and practices, on the part of the books in use, and the almost utter absence of hymns fitted at all to the great seasons of Advent and Epiphany. From November until March, and often at other times, many of our clergymen present, in their sermons, lessons, and prayers, a class of topics which is scarcely touched upon in the hymn-books, and are obliged to sing of other matters, and in other strains, than those which fill the hearts of the people. The true Hymnal must correct this.

The arrangement of the Subjective part should be somewhat more clear, exact, and exhaustive, than we have yet seen. Thus: XIX. The Order of Salvation; A. Invitation; B. Repentance; C. Faith and Justification; D. Peace and Joy. XX. The Christian Life. A. Consecration; B. Sanctification, Outward and Inward; C. Love to God and Christ; D. Trust: 1. In General; 2. In God and Providence; 3. In Christ and Redemption; E. Following Christ; F. Heavenly Spirit; G. Watchfulness and Fidelity; H. Wisdom and Self-knowledge; I. Simplicity and humility; K. Benevolence. XXI. The Cross and Comfort. XXII. Occasions; National, etc. XXIII. Children. XXIV. Private and Family Devotion, Morning and Evening. XXV. Last Things. A. Preparation for Death; B. Burial; C. Resurrection; D. Judgment; E. Heaven.—And last, Doxologies.

Now in the inward part of this,—through those two very extensive and most important heads, the Order of Salvation and the Christian Life,—there should be unity, harmony, and an ascending scale. Repentance should begin with trembling, confession, and woe, close upon the Gospel Call, and gradually rise toward hope and confidence, till its last hymns were hardly distinguishable from the first of Justifying Faith. This again should ascend, from its first agonizing cries, filled yet with oppressive sense of sin, through the comforts and the rest of full belief, till it loses itself in Godly Peace and Joy. It would be delightful to dwell upon the pages of a well constructed Hymnal, where the beauty of the separate contents was doubled by a skilful and complete arrangement, the throbbings of a thousand divinely-led human hearts meeting with and answering each other, the rich experience of different creeds, and lands, and ages, joining, in majestic unison, to pour one tide of solemn grateful song. Now it is meek submission, now fearless constancy : here it utters the trembling notes of half-doubting hope, and presently the eager voice of ardent aspiration : but no discord creeps into the harmony, no passing unworthiness of sense or sound destroys the charm, no feeble break of thought, nor aggressive error of carnal emotion, nor dull defect of language, offends the ear of listeners in heaven or on earth. Our hymn-books ought to be means of grace : but they have commonly been rather proofs of innate depravity. Alas, the dreary distance between the Ideal and the Actual! And yet the Ideal *can* be realized, in no small measure.

As to its *contents*, the true Hymnal should claim some little originality ; or rather it should differ considerably from any other volume in use, or in existence. Probably two-fifths of its material would be new to those who would employ it. The whole number of hymns might be about six hundred : of these, Dr. Watts and Charles Wesley would give about one hundred each, Doddridge and Montgomery some twenty each, Steele, Newton, Cowper, Toplady, Kelly, and John Mason (1683) from ten to fifteen each, and a variety of minor authors from one to eight each. The larger part of the volume would be taken from these familiar sources, though in unfamiliar numbers and proportions. For instance, who has ever yet thought, or dared, to equalize Watts and Wesley? With the Methodists it is all their sweet singer, while all the Calvinists cleave sternly to the Presbyterian muse. *In media veritas.* The true Hymnal shall give to each his due, and divide the apple of discord. Again, we doubt if any one collection ever printed so many as ten hymns from good John Mason, who died fifteen years before Watts began to publish. Yet those ten would be among the brightest, strongest, most intellectual and most devotional poems in the book. We said before that the selection must be unhampered and independent. The compilers should be tied down to no precedents, to no prejudices, to no narrow necessities of the case : whatever seemed sufficiently good should be accepted, whether it were well known or not known at all, from whatsoever source it came,—whatever was adapted, in form, matter, spirit, doctrine, and devotion, to promote the knowledge of truth, the edification of believers, and the glory of the Master: and whatever seemed not so adapted should be thrown aside, no matter what associations might have wound about it, no matter how much some might regret its loss. The compiler should labor after the old Greek motto, and seek to *be best:* with single heart and eye we should go about this work, aiming at the highest, purest, largest, noblest result. And, thus aiming, he will reach certain conclusions which he probably did not at first anticipate. In proportion as the merits of our English hymnology are honestly acknowledged and freely used, its defects will become apparent too. The Ohio compilers, in the preface to their present collection, complain of "our rather barren English hymnology." The accusation, though hardly just, and implying too much, aims at a truth. Our English hymnology is a garden overgrown with weeds and brambles, tangled and in sad confusion, but containing in its mazes many a fruit and flower, some of them beautiful and precious. For a time the eye and taste are satisfied with what grows there; but by-and-by a sameness is perceived, an inadequacy fancied; one cannot live always on the same diet: the taste, educated by experience, longs for viands of simpler flavor and richer substance, more suited to the first wants of appetite and nature, more pure, more nutritious. The present writer is willing to confess that his studies in this department were for several years prosecuted on the loose, unchurchly, merely English basis. He thought that our resources must be found in Watts, Wesley, and the rest of our native hymnists: he had no faith in translations from any other languages, and no idea of introducing any amount of new material, or attempting any radical reform. He now sees that this, which has been the view commonly held, is an error; he sees that this error was with himself, as it is with a very large number of his brethren, simply the result of habit, prejudice and lack of better knowledge: and he says all this about it, because he believes that any man of fair understanding and thorough honesty, who gets a sufficient opportunity of knowing the truth, will come over to it as he has done. This may appear to some a small matter: but it is a very careless or ignorant view that regards it thus. A reform in hymnology will include and produce a corresponding reform everywhere in Church matters.

The deficiencies, then, of our English hymnology have been felt and acknowledged. No subject can be *exhausted;*

but the writer may claim to have attained, for an American, some tolerable knowledge of this. And it is his serious and positive conviction, arrived at deliberately and impartially, after a hearty and admiring study of all that is best in the whole field, that our native English hymns do not fully meet the wants of the Church at this advanced day; that they leave some important Gospel subjects but partially developed, others almost untouched; that for some worthy and great occasions they do not supply us: that some phases of Christ's person and work, and of the relation of these to us, they present most inadequately; and that, with all their beauties and their merits, we want something more. And where shall we look for this additional supply? A voice from God's Word seems to answer: "Stand ye in the ways, and see, and ask for the *old paths*, where is the good way, and walk therein." We have stood in the ways, and seen; what we fail to find around us, we may discover by looking behind. The centuries have been singing God's praises; can we get no help from them? We turn perforce to the Church of our fathers the Reformers, and to the unbroken communion of primitive and mediæval days. The German hymnology is the largest and finest in the world: the Greeks and Latins have their treasures of sacred song. Let us address ourselves to the work, and see what we can get from them. Now hymns made to order are detestable; we cannot, without the divine afflatus, manufacture our own translations, any more than our own originals: the true Hymnal is not produced thus. Therefore we must find what we may, already done to our hand.

And we find more than we could have expected. The Providence of God, answering to the want and desire of the most intelligent portion of English-speaking Christendom, has raised up, within the last thirty years, *translators*, as he raised up original hymnists in the former century. Several gifted and appreciative persons, chiefly members of the Church of England, have produced works of great intrinsic value, and well-adapted to practical use. Some of these have appeared within the last decade; and one, a little volume of rare merit and of exceeding importance, was published but three years ago. From these books our ideal Hymnal of the future, selecting with the same care and taste which it bestowed upon the hymns of native English origin, might gather fifteen or twenty from the *Greek*, chiefly by Dr. Neale; thirty or forty from the *Latin*, by Chandler,

Caswall, Neale, and others; and near one hundred from the *German,* half of them by Miss Winkworth, the rest from John Wesley, Miss Cox, "Hymns from the Land of Luther," and several minor sources. Some of these translations would be found to have all the force and grace of noble original poems, all to be smooth and respectable. It might take people some little time to get accustomed to the new atmosphere, the tone of thought and feeling, somewhat different from the body of our English hymns: but whoever overcame the first strangeness, would see and feel the exquisite beauty, the earnest solemnity, the greater solidity and purity, the deeper experience, the juster views, the healthier and completer piety, the general *satisfactoriness* of these, as above and against the common run of our English hymns, even some of those which the same book would contain. It is impossible to study these German, Greek, and Latin, hymns at all fully and impartially, even through the medium of translations, without gaining a deep admiration and affection for them, and a consequent distaste and discontent with much that we are forced to sing now. Not only are they so much simpler, purer, sweeter, but often we must see that they have *the truth,* when our English lyrics are in error. Let the true Hymnal lead us back, then, joyfully, to the good old ways.

Every collection of mark and merit published during the last ten years, then, will be found to contain a greater or less infusion of translations from the German and the Latin: and nearly every hymn-book that has happened within that time, whatever its origin, and character, shows something of the prevailing turn and taste. We find this not only in the Episcopal Church, where we might expect it, but among Presbyterians, Congregationalists, Baptists, and Methodists. The selections are not always made with great care or taste, and do not often show thorough knowledge of the field: but they unmistakably indicate the direction which the hymnologic investigation of the day is taking. It would appear, also, from what these compilers have done as it is, that had they been more familiar with the large number of translated hymns recently added to our literature, their selections therefrom would have been larger. But to our figures.

In Andrews' "Hymns and Devotional Poetry," (Low Church Episcopal,) 1857. 460 hymns. There are 21 from the German and 7 from the Latin. "Hymns for Church and Home," (Episcopal,) 1860. 417 hymns. 20 are German and 29 Latin. In Dr. Boardman's Supplement to the Old

School Presbyterian Psalms and Hymns, of 510, 28 are German and 32 Latin. In Dana's Collection, (Presbyterian,) Charleston, 1860, of 491 hymns, 14 are from the German, 15 from the Latin, and 1 from the Syriac. In Robinson's "Songs of the Church," (Presbyterian,) 1862. 1,193 hymns. 16 are German and 9 Latin. In the Sabbath Hymn-Book, (Congregational,) 1858. Of 1,290, at least 40 are German, 24 Latin, and 2 Greek. Dr. Adams' "Church Pastorals," (Congregational,) Boston, 1864. 988 hymns, has 24 German and 17 Latin. Mr. Beecher's Plymouth Hymn-Book ; 1855, has, of 1,374 pieces, at least 23 German and 17 Latin. "Hymns for the Church of Christ, by Drs. Hedge and Huntington, (High Arian,) 1853, of 886, 33 are German, 34 Latin, and 1 Greek. (This was two years before the first volume of Lyra Germanica.) Of the 159 hymns annexed to Dr. Osgood's "Christian Worship,"(Unitarian,) New York, 1862. 5 are German and 19 Latin. One or two German Reformed compilations, which we have not by us, contain a number of German translations. We might add, as corresponding testimony from across the water, that the present hymn-book of the English Congregational Union, 1855, of 1,000 hymns has at least 18 German and 10 Latin. Paxton Hood's Brighton Hymn-book, (Congregational,) 1862, of 230, has 8 from the German. In the collection put forth by the Young Men's Christian Association, London, 1862, of 562 hymns, 16 are German. A majority of these books are compiled by, and for, people who care nothing for the Festivals, for the distinctively objective presentation of Christian truth, for the Churchly System as a whole, or in any of its parts : people who probably did not feel, in any considerable measure, the deficiencies of our English hymnology, and who took this German and Latin material, as they would have taken anything else, simply on its own intrinsic merits.

If we turn to the Church of England, we shall find testimony of another sort. A very active and interesting movement has been going on there for some years, which has effected great change in the hymnology of the mother country, and gone far to produce among us the result indicated by the statistics above given. There is a strong reaction towards the old ways : a great number of hymns have been produced, which are either translated from the Latin, or written on the basis and after the style of the old Latin models ; and there is a tendency to use these largely or chiefly. Many of these new-old pieces do possess unusual merit.

The Ecclesiological Society's Hymnal, 1856, contains 105 hymns, *all* from the Latin. Of Oldknow's "Hymns for the Service of the Church," Birmingham, 1854, 163 in number, 130 are Latin. Skinner's Daily Service Hymnal, the last edition, 1864, has 310 hymns, of which 125 are from the Latin, and 22 from the Greek. The famous "Hymns Ancient and Modern," of which a million and a half copies are said to have been issued, which has been adopted by the British Admiralty, for use in all the vessels in her Majesty's service, and has made its way into Caffrania and Madagascar, consists of 273 pieces, from one-third, to one-half of which are of Latin origin, and several more of German. Lord Nelson's Salisbury Hymnal, which had some time since reached a circulation of 80,000, is of similar proportions. So is a "Selection of Hymns for Public and Private Use," 1847. Nor is this large proportion of foreign matter found only in distinctively High Church publications. The Collection of the Society for Promoting Christian Knowledge (300 hymns, published at two pence) contains a number from the Latin: as in many of the other books, they are not indicated, and we have not stopped to distinguish and count them. And in Mercer's Church Psalter and Hymn-Book, 1859, (Mr. Mercer was James Montgomery's pastor during the poet's later years) of 510 hymns, while but 9 appear to be Latin, 40 are from the German.

Now can we not learn something from all this? We have no right to say, "These men are not of our way of thinking, we have no concern with them." The wise disciple, while he calls no man his master but Christ, is willing to own some sympathy with any of his brethren, and to accept some instruction from each. The true Hymnal will slavishly follow none, but will study all, and then strike out for itself what seems the right path.

We have only one thing more to say, and that concerns the spirit, tone, feeling, of the ideal Hymn-book. We would have a book with more force, fervor, passion, poetry, than perhaps any one volume that we know: with more genuine feeling and experience than any hymn-book now extant: a book most thoroughly and intensely human. Only it should put this human element in the right place, and use it in the right way. It should distinguish between the false and the true, between real religion and the things that may happen to really religious people. It would not present vulgar crudities, love-sick fancies, and discontented murmurs, as legiti-

mate products of the Holy Spirit. But, after throwing aside
the vast mass of inferior and faulty matter with which our
hymn-books are yet loaded, it would retain abundance of
earnest feeling and tender human interest; it would still be
able to express, with a richness of variety, purity, and depth
unknown before, the thanksgivings and petitions, the strifes
and fears, the resolution and endeavors, the beliefs and long-
ings, the joys and hopes, of every well-instructed believer,
every right-minded child of God on earth.

We have said enough. Should such a book appear, its
path would not be one of roses. Some would be suspicious
of its origin, others of its objects; many would not compre-
hend its plan and spirit and scope, the ends it was meant to
serve, the principles which would underlie it. But others,
more liberal or more enlightened, must see that of such a
book there is sad and positive need, and that it might become
a great agent—none greater—for the spread among us of
pure doctrine and correct usage, the revival of just views,
principles, practices, the regeneration of our Zion in this land.
Then may the true Hymnal soon appear, and may God's
blessing be upon it long!

ARTICLE III.

THE SABBATH, A DELIGHT.

By Joseph A. Seiss, D, D., Philadelphia, Pa.

There is a Psalm, the ninety-second, which bears the
title: "The Sabbath Day." The authorship of this Psalm
has been variously stated. Some ascribe it to Adam in
Eden, some to Moses, and others to David. It is hardly to
be supposed, however, that Adam was beset in Paradise
with the workers of iniquity, and the troublesome enemies,
of whom this Psalm speaks; or, that either Adam or Moses
had at hand the psalteries, harps and instruments of music,
with which this devout singer found it so good to show forth
the loving-kindness of the Lord. If tradition ought to yield
to the force of internal evidences, the great majority of in-

terpreters are right in ascribing this, as most of the Psalms, to Israel's royal singer, the son of Jesse. But, whoever may have been its author, it is agreed, that it is an inspired production, and that the title which it bears is a part of it. By divine authority, it is a *"Song for the Sabbath-day."* From this Psalm we may, consequently, learn, in what light to regard the institution of the Sabbath; what that is which accords best with its design; and how a heart under the control of the Holy Spirit, is affected with regard to it. That which is the subject or occasion for song, is a matter of gladness and rejoicing. Singing most naturally connects with joy and pleasure. David continually associates it with emotions of worship, exultation, triumph, peace and hope. We never sing because we are sad. Dirge-like lamentations are not unknown to sacred psalmody; but when the Scriptures urge us to sing, it is never for sorrow or distress, but for joy and gladness. When God's ancient people were in affliction, they hung their harps upon the willows, and said, *"How can we sing?"* According to the apostle, grief calls for prayer; but, "Is any *merry?* let him *sing."*

If the Sabbath-day, then, is a time for song, and if God has inspired and appointed songs for that particular day, we are not only authorized, but required, to regard it as designed to be a day of delight, at least to the truly devout. A day for singing, is a glad day, joyous day, a happy day; and as such I propose, at present, to consider the holy Sabbath-day.

I use the word *Sabbath* in its wider and less particular sense. There are some Christians who are reluctant to apply the term *Sabbath*, to the day kept holy by the Christian Church. They think it savors too much of Judaism and legal ceremonies. They prefer to speak of "The Lord's Day," or *Sunday.* I have no controversy with any on these points, though I think *Sabbath* a name quite as Scriptural and appropriate. It means *rest;* and the *Sabbath-day* is simply the sacred *Rest-day,* including as well the seventh, on which it anciently fell, as the first, on which it is observed since the time of Christ. I know of no more necessary connection of the word with Jewish ceremonies, than the word *Sunday* has with heathenism. And if John does speak of "the Lord's Day;" Paul, in a passage quite as pertinent, speaks of a σαββατισμος—a *Sabbath keeping,* which still remains to the people of God. The ceremonial regulations, with which the Sabbath was surrounded in the Mosaic ritual, have passed away; but the *Rest-day,* the devotion to sacred purposes of

THE

EVANGELICAL

QUARTERLY REVIEW.

EDITED BY

M. L. STOEVER,

Professor in Pennsylvania College.

———◆———

VOLUME XVI.

———◆◆◆———

GETTYSBURG:

AUGHINBAUGH & WIBLE, BOOK & JOB PRINTERS,

CHAMBERSBURG STREET, SECOND SQUARE.

1865.

CONTENTS OF NO. LXI.

This ably conducted organ of the Lutheran Church contains for the present quarter: The Wisdom of the World and of the Church compared; Dr. Kurtz's Instruction in Evangelical Lutheran Doctrine; Study of the Ancient Classics; German Language; Deceased Lutheran Ministers; Precious Stones; Lord's Supper; Catechisation; Mystical Union; Responsibilities of the American Citizen; New Publications.—*American Presbyterian.*

It is, as usual, full of valuable matter, some of it unique, and not likely to be found elsewhere.—*Congregationalist.*

The Evangelical Review contains The Wisdom of the World and of the Church compared, by F. W. Conrad, D. D. The author illustrates in an impressive manner the truth of the saying that "the children of this world in their generation are wiser than the children of light." It is a stirring appeal to the Lutheran Church, to arouse from her lethargy and act truly, and a luminous exposition of the way in which this may be done. The study of the Ancient Classics, by Charles Short, A. M., is a good argument in favor of the study of the Ancient Languages, and of classical studies in general; The German Language, by Prof. J. W. Nevin. D. D., written in Dr. Nevin's usual nervous style, is a merited enconium upon the German Language, showing the importance of studying it. Reminiscences of Deceased Lutheran Ministers continues the interesting series of Memoirs of departed Lutheran Ministers, the present number being devoted to Rev. Charles A. Baer. Precious Stones and the Lord's Supper are translations from Zeller's Wörterbach, executed with the skill which we are accustomed to expect from Dr. Schaeffer and Prof. Muhlenberg; Catechisation, by Rev. Thomas Lape, A. M. There are some good points in this article on a very important subject. As the next number begins a new volume, now is a good time to subscribe for the *Quarterly.*—*Lutheran Standard.*

The Editor has presided over the pages of the *Review* with singular impartiality, great judiciousness and commendable zeal. Such services deserve the lasting gratitude, and call for the necessary co-operation on the part of the Church.—*Lutheran Observer.*

We cannot over estimate the importance of the *Review* to the Church, or insist too strongly on the necessity of effort on the part of its friends to extend its circulation during these depressing times. Prof. Stoever would deserve the thanks of the whole Church, if he did no more than keep the *Review* in being, but he has left nothing undone to give it life, variety and interest, and his success has been proportioned to his care.—*Luth. & Miss.*

CONTENTS OF NO. LXII.

This Number opens Vol. XVI. Professor Stoever announces the raising of the price of the *Review* to $3 per annum. This would have been little enough, even in the best times. To ask it now surely requires no apology. Mr. Bird's very thorough and able article on Lutheran Hymnology will be read with great interest and its continuation eagerly looked for. He is *facile princeps* among the rising Hymnologists and his labors, if his life be spared to complete them, will create a treasure house of sacred song, and its love for the whole Christian Church. The discussion of the name Jehovah by Professor Green, is worthy of the subject, and the ripe scholarship of its author. Another able article, by a writer, not of our Church, is the exposure of the hollowness of Darwin's theory of species, by Rev. E. F. Williams. Professor Stoever has had remarkable success in securing the co öperation of good writers in the larger world of theology and literature, and has given us some of the best things from the best pens. The articles of Dr. Brown, Rev. M. Valentine and Rev. J. H. W. Stuckenberg are very good, each in its kind. Mr. Traver's article on "Repose as an Element of Christian Character," is original, carefully wrought out and suggestive. Professor Stoever gives us one of his characteristically valuable and seasonable articles, in which the leading facts and statistics in regard to Pennsylvania College are brought together. Dr. Kurtz closes the list of contributors with an article in which he gives some very sensible views on American Slavery, prefacing them with a discussion of the borrowing from the Egyptians.—*Lutheran & Missionary.*

This is an unusually rich Number. We need not analyze its contents closely for it is, or ought to be, in every intelligent Lutheran's hand. We note with pleasure that the indefatigable Editor, Professor Stoever, has added to the interest of this volume by valuable contributions from pens, outside the Church. Professor Green's article will be carefully read. Professor Brown's paper is a plain, vigorous setting forth of his subject. Mr. Bird's article on the Hymnology of our Church is full of curious information and racy criticism. Mr. Valentine's paper is an impressive appeal to the ministry, well worthy of careful consideration. We thank the author of Pennsylvania College for interesting details and statistics. It is a paper to be preserved and referred to.—*Lutheran Observer.*

Professor Stoever deserves credit for the ability with which he gets up the *Review*. The present is an admirable Number, containing some articles of great and permanent value.—*Lutheran Standard.*

The *Evangelical Review* for January has made its appearance. So far as we have examined the Number, it is a very interesting one.—*American Lutheran.*

The *Evangelical Review* is edited by Professor Stoever, with distinguished zeal and great devotion to the good cause. The fifteen volumes of the *Review*, which have already appeared we value highly as the most valuable treasure of the English part of our Church in this country. No other Lutheran work in the English language, can be compared with it.—*"Zeitschrift."*

The January Number of this *Quarterly* is one of much interest. The work continues to be ably edited by Professor Stoever, and it speaks well for the energy and activity of the Lutheran Church, that it is still sustained under all the pressure of the times.—*German Reformed Messenger.*

A valuable Number with a great variety in the articles, and on subjects of present interest. A high tone of evangelical piety pervades the *Review*. The terms although raised are but $3 per annum.—*American Presbyterian.*

CONTENTS OF NO. LXII.

The *Evangelical Quarterly Review* for April, is confessedly a number of unusual interest. Its matter may be thus classified : I. Translations. Dr. Schmucker gives us a valuable translation of Luthardt's Two Generic Aspects of the World; Rev. G. A. Wenzel has admirably translated from Sartorius' Holy Love an article "Of God," characterized by the earnest devoutness and profundity of that great writer; Professor Muhlenberg renders an instructive article on "Elders," from Zeller's Bible Dictionary. II. *Articles for the Times.*—Dr. Conrad on "The Hand of God in the War," is very seasonable, and one of the best articles he has ever written. Dr. Ziegler discourses of "Politics and the Pulpit," with his characteristic, plain, manly good sense. He takes his position thoughtfully, presses his argument with luminous judgment, and establishes them almost beyond cavil. "The Christian Commission," bears internal evidence, we think, of coming from the hand of that active and esteemed co-worker with the Commission Professor Stoever, the Editor of the Review. It is a general survey, both of the principles and of the work of the Commission, and is a very interesting, useful and well timed sketch. III. *Sacred Belles-Lettres.*—Dr. Brown's article on the "Poetry of the Bible," is discriminating and good. His remarks upon his Biblical Parallelism, and his illustrations of the same element in modern literature, are specially valuable. The Article of the number which will attract most readers and excite most feeling is, "Lutheran Hymnology," by Rev. F. M. Bird. It is thorough, rich in biographical and curious detail in regard to a thousand points of interest, on which Mr. Bird's labors are the first to shed light. Every reader of the *Review* will look anxiously for the continuation of the Article.—*Lutheran & Missionary.*

The translation from Luthardt, by Dr. Schmucker, is interesting as revealing the intense bitterness of a ministry against the religion of Christ that exists in the minds of the free-thinkers of Germany. Dr. Conrad with a bold, fiery rhetoric, depicts the evident working of God's hand in our national struggle. Professor Ziegler demolishes with irrevocable logic and pitiless proof, the flimsy position that religion has nothing to do with politics. He shows from Scripture, past the possibility of a cavil, that God is not excluded from the State, and that his message is to rulers and citizens, that the pulpit not only has a right, but is bound to lay down the law of God respecting the duties of citizens. Professor Brown's paper on the Poetry of the Bible, is all the more pleasing because it evinces, that he can wield the pen of the ready writer as well in the field of rhetoric as in the domain of logic.—*Lutheran Observer.*

"*The Evangelical Quarterly Review,*" for April, is on our table, filled as usual, with valuable and interesting matter. "The Hand of God in ·the War," by F. W. Conrad, D. D.; "Politics and the Pulpit," by Prof. Henry Ziegler; and the "Poetry of the Bible," by Prof. J. A. Brown, D. D., look more entertaining, and have been marked for future reading. Professor Stoever furnishes his readers in this number with an interesting and ably written article on "The United States Christian Commission," showing its origin and the great work it has accomplished and the good resulting therefrom. The liberal spirit on which the *Review* is conducted, and the loyal tone which characterizes its pages, should commend it to the favor of an intelligent public.—*Star & Banner.*

The Evangelical Quarterly Review. This periodical is published in Gettysburg and devoted to the exposition and defence of the doctrines of the Evangelical Lutheran Church. The April number before us is very interesting. The articles entitled "The Hand of God in the War," "Politics and the Pulpit," and the "United States Christian Commission," are exceedingly able and satisfactory articles, and we are sorry that their length forbids their transfer to our columns.—*Juniata Sentinel.*

CONTENTS OF NO. LXIV.

The Evangelical Quarterly Review for July contains: The Evangelical Doctrine of Ordination, by Prof. Loy; Lutheran Hymnology, by Rev. F. M. Bird ; The Sabbath a Delight, by Rev. Dr. Seiss ; Ministers of the Gospel, the Moral Watchmen of Nations, by Rev. Dr. Conrad ; "Know Thyself," Personally and Nationally Considered, by Hon. Edward McPherson; Abraham Lincoln; Installation Addresses, the Charge, by Rev. B. M. Schmucker, and the Reply by Rev. Dr. C. P. Krauth, Jr. Several of the articles are characterized by high literary excellence, and we shall endeavor to find room for extracts.—*New York Evangelist.*

This *Quarterly* is published at Gettysburg under the auspices of the Evangelical Lutheran Church, and is edited by Professor Stoever. The July number contains eight articles, including the usual notices of recent publications. Whilst the greater portion of the articles are denominational, there is still food, also, for the outside reader.—*German Reformed Messenger.*

This is an excellent number. The article on "Hymnology" is as full of interest, as its predecessors. Dr. Seiss on the "Sabbath" puts forth his usual power and eloquence. Dr. Conrad handles his subject, "Ministers of the Gospel, the Moral Watchmen of the Nations," like a master. Mr. McPherson's article is original, ingenious and striking. The article on "Abraham Lincoln" is a most valuable contribution.—*Lutheran Observer.*

The July No. of this *Quarterly* has reached us with its customary promptness. The number is an interesting one, and although from the plan of the work, our ministers could not expect to agree with all that it offers, we do not see how they can well get along without it.—*Lutheran Standard.*

The Evangelical Quarterly Review, (July,) opens with an able and learned article by Professor Loy on the Lutheran Doctrine of Ordination. The second article closes Mr. Bird's wholly unique and masterly discussion of Lutheran Hymnology. Dr. Seiss presents the Sabbath as a Delight, in a very admirable and practical manner. Dr. Conrad exhibits Ministers of the Gospel, as the Moral Watchmen of Nations. The Hon. Edward McPherson with his characteristic philosophical thoughtfulness considers the proposition "Know Thyself," in its application to persons and nations. The main contribution of the Editor, Professor Stoever, to the number is a full and appreciative exhibition of the life, services and character of our noble and lamented President. The seventh article embraces the Charge of Rev. B. M. Schmucker and the Reply made to it at the Installation of the Professors, October 4th, 1864.—*Lutheran & Missionary.*

The Evangelical Quarterly Review for July is already out. The present number seems to be better than any preceding it. Hon. Edward McPherson, contributes "Know Thyself," written in the author's usual vigorous style. It is worth a careful perusal. The article on Abraham Lincoln, by Prof. Stoever, runs through twenty-two pages, and is a just tribute to our martyr-President. It is interesting throughout and can be read with much profit.—*Gettysburg Star.*

www.ingramcontent.com/pod-product-compliance
Lightning Source LLC
Chambersburg PA
CBHW032245080426
42735CB00008B/1010